William James Stavert

# The Register of St. Mary's Chapel at Conistone,

in the Parish of Burnsall-in-Craven 1567-1812

William James Stavert

**The Register of St. Mary's Chapel at Conistone,**
*in the Parish of Burnsall-in-Craven 1567-1812*

ISBN/EAN: 9783337430375

Printed in Europe, USA, Canada, Australia, Japan

Cover: Foto ©Suzi / pixelio.de

More available books at **www.hansebooks.com**

# THE REGISTER OF

# ST. MARY'S CHAPEL

AT

# CONISTONE,

IN THE PARISH OF

# BURNSALL-IN-CRAVEN,

# 1567—1812.

EDITED BY

W. J. STAVERT, M.A.,

RECTOR OF BURNSALL, YORKS, AND

CHAPLAIN TO THE EARL OF CRAVEN.

SKIPTON:

PRINTED AT THE "CRAVEN HERALD" OFFICE, HIGH STREET.

1894.

CURTA SUPELLEX.

1356225

REVERENDISSIMO

IN DEO PATRI

IOHANNI

PERMISSIONE DIVINA

DOMINO EPISCOPO RICHMONDENSI

PASTORI VERE NOSTRO

D.

# ADVERTISEMENT.

This book contains all that is known to exist of the Conistone Register down to and including the year 1812. The records are contained in four books: A having 12 leaves, in size 14 × 6½ inches; B 9 leaves, 15 × 7½ inches; C 7 leaves, 22½ × 12 inches; and D 16 leaves, 15 × 10 inches. In all save the last the entries have been made on parchment. There are, as will appear, a few gaps, and in binding the chronological order has not always been followed. The copy aims at being an exact reproduction of the original in every respect, dotted lines being used where the MS. is illegible, and square brackets where anything has been interlineated or added to the context by a later hand.

Much of the first register book is quite illegible by the ordinary reader, and its transcription has given the writer not a little trouble.

Nomina sponsaliu' Anno Regni Reginæ Elizabethæ nono. [A fol. 1. r.

Willya' Broadbelt and Hellen warde were married the vij$^{th}$ day of Julye.

John Tennante & Elizabeth Ellisse were married the xx$^{th}$ day of Julye.

Roger Hartlay & Margret Hodgsonn were marryed the third day of Auguste.

Nomina defunctoru' code' Anno.

Margret Tennant was buryed the xv$^{th}$ day of May.

Alexander winterburne was buryed the xxviij day of September.

Alice Horner was buryed the iiij$^{th}$ day of Januarie.

Nomina pueroru' baptizandoru' Anno Regni Reginæ Eliz: 12.

Margrett the daughter of John Battie was baptized Januarie the xxix$^{th}$

Hellen the daughter of Myles Laylande was bap: Februarie the fyrst.

Gennet the daughter of John Tennant was bap: March the xij$^{th}$

Nomina pueroru' baptizandoru' Anno Regni Reginæ Eliz: 13$^{th}$

Edwarde the sonne of Anthonie warde was baptized Nouember the iiij$^{th}$

Henry the sonne of Robert Ibbotsonn was baptized Apryll the viij$^{th}$

Agnes the daughter of Christofer Settle was bap: May the xx$^{th}$

Gennet the daughter of Thomas Winterburne was bap: June the third.

Hellen the daughter of Thomas Laylande was bap: July the xv$^{th}$

Lawrence the sonne of Myles Laylande was bap: August the xix$^{th}$

Nomina defunctoru' code' anno.

Hellen Laylande was buryed Februarie the ix$^{th}$

John Drake was buryed Januarie the xxv$^{th}$

Alice Garforth was buryed March the xiiij$^{th}$

Gennet Bow was buryed Januarie the xiij$^{th}$

Alice Lambart was buryed Feb: the xj$^{th}$

John Pearsonn was buryed Februarie the xvij$^{th}$

Jeffray Kydd was buryed Aprill the xvj$^{th}$

Margret Costentyne was buryed June the vj$^{th}$

Margret Garforth was buryed August the xxv$^{th}$

Nomina sponsaliu' code' anno.

Thomas Parkinsonn & Hellen Laylande were marryd July the fyrst.

Nomina pueroru' batizandoru' Anno Reg: Reginæ Eliz: 14$^{to}$

Hellen the daughter of Thomas Ibbotsonn was bap: Nouember the xx$^{th}$

Roberte the sonne of Willya' Broadbelt was bap: Nouember the xxv$^{th}$

Hellen the daughter of Roger Franckland was bap: Januarie the xx$^{th}$

Thomas the sonne of John Pearesonn was bap: December the xix$^{th}$

Margret the daughter of John Tennant was bap: Januarie the xxvij$^{th}$

Anne the daughter of Richard Fawcett was bap: Februarie the xxiiij$^{th}$

Gennet the daughter of Willya Broadbelt was bap: July the xxvj$^{th}$

Jeane the daughter of Richard Settle was bap: August the tenth.

Nomina defunctoru' code' anno.

Issabell Laylande was buryed the xviij$^{th}$ day of Januarie.

Richard Gawthroppe was buryed the xxv$^{th}$ day of Februarie.

Alice Ibbotsonn was buryed the xij$^{th}$ day of Februarie.
Margaret Lawsonn was buryed the xix$^{th}$ day of Februarie.
Henry Laylande was buryed the xii$^{th}$ day of March.
Thomas Kydde was buryed the xxv$^{th}$ day of March.
Alice Battie was buryed the xxvij$^{th}$ of Apryll.
Leonard Kydd was buryed the xxx$^{th}$ day of Maye.
Robert Battie was buryed the xxv$^{th}$ day of June.

Nomina sponsaliu' eode' Anno.

Robert wigglesworth and Margret Lambert were married June the viij$^{th}$
Lawrence Tutin & Elizabeth Hodgsonn were Marryed June the xiiij$^{th}$
Richard Settle & Margrett Costentyne were marryed June the xxiij$^{th}$
Costan Bantonn Gennet Settle were marryed the xxix$^{th}$ of June.
Richard Clarke & Issabell Richardsonn were marryed the xj of Julie.
John Speake & Alice Slinger were marryed the ix$^{th}$ day of Auguste.

Nomina pueroru' baptizandoru' Anno Regni Reginæ Elizabethæ 15°

Richard the sonne of George Horner was baptized Februarie the xv$^{th}$
Roberte the sonne of Thomas Drake was bap: March the xv$^{th}$
Thomas the sonne of Anthonie Warde was bap: March the xvj$^{th}$
Elizabeth the daughter of Thomas Hodgson was bap: Apryll the x$^{th}$

Nomina pueoru' baptiz: anno p^r^dicto. [A fol. 1. v.

Anne the daughter of Henry Garforth was bap: Aprill the xxv$^{th}$
Hellen the daughter of Robert Settle was bap: May the fyrst.
John the sonne of Jefray Costentyne was baptized May the xxv$^{th}$
Richard the sonne of John Battie was baptized Julie the fyfte.
John the sonne of John Laylande was bap: the second day of August.
John the sonne of Thomas Ibbotsonn was bap: September the xiij$^{th}$

Nomina defunctoru' Anno p^r^dicto.

Agnes warde was buryed the fyrst day of December.
Emmot Settle was buryed the xxvj$^{th}$ day of March.
Roberte Laylande was buryed the xviij$^{th}$ day of Julie.
Roberte Battie was buryed the seconde day of September.
Agnes Francklande was buryed the xviij$^{th}$ day of March.

Nomina defunctoru' Anno Regni Reginæ Elizabethæ 16$^{to}$

Issabell Pottertonn was buryed the xviij$^{th}$ day of December.
Willyam Lawsonn was buryed the xx$^{th}$ day of December.
Willyam Lambart was buryed the xx$^{th}$ day of December.
John Picall was buried the xvj$^{th}$ day of Apryll.
Anthonie Garforth was buryed the xj$^{th}$ day of Maye.
Margret Abrahã was buryed the ix$^{th}$ day of June.

Nomina pueroru' baptizandoru' eode' Anno.

Issabell the daughter of Thomas Settle was bap: Januarie the xxx$^{th}$
Issabell the daughter of Thomas Laylande was bap: Februarie the xxij$^{th}$
George the sonne of George Tennant was bap: Apryll the xxv$^{th}$
Henry the sonne of Richard Thompsonn was bap: May the ix$^{th}$
Hellen the daughter of willya' Battie was bap: May the xxiij$^{th}$

Hellen the daughter of Thomas winterburne was bap : July the xv^th^
Henry the sonne of Myles Layland was bap : August the viij^th^
willya' the sonne of Robert wiggleswoorth was bap : September y^e^ xxv^th^
willya' the sonne of Thomas Lambart was bap : September the xxviij^th^
Issabell the daughter of Robert Settle was bap : October the xx^th^
Henry the sonne of Thomas Ibbotsonn was bap : Nouember the xiiij^th^
Edwarde the sonne of willya' Broadbelt was bap : Januarie the ij^th^
Anthonie the sonne of Anthonie warde was bap : March the xxv^th^
Agnes the daughter of Roger Touler was bap : March the fyfte.

Nomina sponsaliu' eode' anno.

Christofer Ellisse & Issabell Broadbelt were marryed Aprill y^e^ xxiij^th^
Richard Iueson & Agnes Pecow were marryed June the fyfte.

nomina puerorn' baptiz : Anno Regni Reginæ Eliz : 18^to^

Marie the daughter of Richard Thompsonn bap : December the xiij^th^
Henry the sonne of Robert Settle was bap : October the xiij^th^
Thomas the sonne of Robert wiggleswoorth was bap : August the xxx^th^
John the sonne of Richard Iuesonn was bap : March the xj^th^
Jane the daughter of Henry Garforth was bap : Nouember the iiij^th^
Issabell the daughter of John Pearsonn was bap : May the vj^th^
Alice the daughter of John Tennante was bap : June the xvij^th^
Margret the daughter of Thomas Lambart was bap : June y^e^ xviij^th^
John the sonne of Thomas Settle was bap : June the xix^th^
Willya' the sonne of Thomas Drake was bap : June xix^th^
Hellen the daughter of Richard Settle was bap : Julye y^e^ xv^th^
Margret the daughter of Robert Ibbotsonn was bap : Julie the xxj^th^
Thomas the sonne of Anthonie Kydd was bap : August the xv^th^
Anne the daughter of Richard Layland was bap : August the fyrst.

Nomina defunctoru' Anno Reg Reginæ Elizabethæ 18^to^ [A fol. 2. r.

John Kydde was buryed Aprill the xj^th^
John Lambart was buryed Auguste the xx^th^
Margret Thompsonn was buryed Auguste the xxx^th^
Richard wiggleswoorth was buryed September the seconde.

Nomina sponsaliu' eode' anno.

Anthonie Kydd & Anne Richardsonn were marryed June the vij^th^

Nomina sponsaliu' anno Reg. Reginæ Elizabethæ 19^to^

George Ripplay & Anne Costentyne were marryed June the ix^th^
Thomas Rathmell & Margret Hebdenn were marryed June the xix^th^
Leonard Lofthouse & Gennet Bantonn were marryed September y^e^ viij^th^

Nomina pueroru' baptiz : eode' anno.

Henry the sonne of Thomas Hodgsonn was bap : December the xx^th^
Thomas the sonne of willya' Battie was bap : Januarie the xxvij^th^
Gennet the daughter of the sayd willya' Battie was bap : the same day.
George the sonne of Anthonie warde was bap : March the x^th^
Alice the daughter of Thomas Ibbotsonn was bap : March the xxiiij^th^
Gennett the daughter of Anthony Kydd was bap : Aprill the xix^th^
Henry the sonne of John Laylande was bap : May the fyrst.
Alice the daughter of Henry Loynde was bap : May the xxvj^th^

John the sonne of Thomas Laylande was bap: June the xxv$^{th}$
Thomas the sonne of Roger Touler was bap: July the vij$^{th}$
Margret the daughter of Willya' Broadbelt was bap: December y$^{e}$ xxj$^{th}$
Frances the daughter of John Mydlam was bap: October the xxvij$^{th}$
Thomas the sonne of Roger Franckland was bap: December the xx$^{th}$
Issabell the daughter of Myles Layland March the xvij$^{th}$

Nomina defunctoru' eode' Anno.

Alice Stapper was buryed the fyrst day of December.
Thomas winterburne was buryed the xiiij$^{th}$ day of Januarie.
Christofer Tennante was buryed the xxiiijth day of Januarie.
Agnes Battie was buryed the syxt day of Apryll.
willya' Battie was buryed the tenth day of Apryll.
Alice Todd was buryed the xxx$^{th}$ day of May.
Richard Battie was buried the xix$^{th}$ day of June.
John Settle was buried September the xxiij$^{th}$
Gennet Lofthouse was buryed October the fyrst.
Robert Costentyne was buryed October the vij$^{th}$
Thomas Iuesonn was buryed October the vij$^{th}$
Leonard Hebdenn was buryed October the xiiij$^{th}$
Hellen Settle was buryed Nouember the fyfte.
Frances Mydlam was buryed December the xiiij$^{th}$
Thomas Franckland was buryed March the fyrst.

Nomina defunctoru' Anno Regni Reginæ Elizabethæ 20$^{mo}$

Thomas Franckland was buryed March the tenth.
Issabell Franckland was buryed May the fyrst.
Alice Tennante was buryed December the xix$^{th}$

Nomina puероru' baptizandoru' eodem Anno.

Hellen the daughter of Richard Settle was bap August xvij$^{th}$
John the son of Robert Settle was bap: Nouember the xxx$^{th}$
Thomas the sonne of Anthonie Kydd was bap December the xxj$^{th}$
Grace the daughter of Robert wiggleswoorth Januarie the xxx$^{th}$

Nomina sponsaliu' eode' anno.

John Bolland & Hellen Battie were marryed June the fyrst.
willya' Todde & Margret Faldshaw were marryed June the viij$^{th}$
willya' Deane & Effa' Laylande were marryed June the xxvj$^{th}$
Myles Knowles and Margret Costentyne wer marryed July y$^{e}$ vj$^{th}$

Nomina defunctoru' Anno Eliz. R. Reg. 21$^{mo}$

Lawrence Costentyne was buryed Februarie the viij$^{th}$
willya' Drake was buryed Februarie the xx$^{th}$
Margret Marshon was buryed Apryll the xxx$^{th}$
Alice wiggleswoorth was buryed May the viij$^{th}$
Grace wiggleswoorth was buryed May the xxij$^{th}$
Roger wiggleswoorth was buried June the ix$^{th}$
Robert Costentyne was buryed August the vij$^{th}$

Nomina pueroru' baptiz anno p$^{r}$dicto.

John the sonne of Henry Garforth was baptized Apryll the xiij$^{th}$
Elizabeth the daughter of Robert Thompsonn was baptized May the xiij$^{th}$

Anno p$^{r}$dicto. [A fol. 2. v.

Roberte the sonne of Jeffray Costentyne was baptized June the second.
Margret & Dorethie the daughters of Richard Laylund were bap: August y$^{e}$ ij$^{th}$
Grace the daughter of Tomas Settle was bap: August the seconde.
Grace the daughter of Roberte Ibbotsonn was bap: August the ix$^{th}$
Gennet the daughter of Thomas Kydd was bap: August the xxxiij$^{th}$
Thomas the sonne of Richard Thompsonn was bap: September the xiij$^{th}$
Mathew the sonne of Anthonie Warde was bap: September the xxj$^{th}$
Gennet the daughter of Thomas Lambart was bap: Nouember the viij$^{th}$
Peter the sonne of Robert Wiggleswoorth was bap: June the xxix$^{th}$

Nomina sponsaliu' eode' Anno.

Willya' Slinger & Elizabeth Settle were marryed June the xxj$^{th}$

Nomina puerorū' baptizandor' Anno Reg. Reginæ Eliz: 22$^{do}$

Issabell the daughter of Thomas Drake was baptized Nouember the xxij$^{th}$
Isabell & Alice the daughters of Willya' Broadbelt were bap: Januarie y$^{e}$ xvj$^{th}$
Richard the sonne of Willya' Todde was bap: Januarie the xxj$^{th}$
Elizabeth the daughter of James Rayner was bap: februarie the xxvij$^{th}$
Thomas the sonne of Thomas Ibbotsonn was bap: May the xxix$^{th}$
Willya' the sonne of Thomas Nowell was bap: August the xxviij$^{th}$
Christopher the sonne of Anthonie Kydd was bap: September the xxj$^{th}$
Alice the daughter of Thomas Laylande was bap: September the xxv$^{th}$
Thomas the sonne of Robert Settle was bap: October the seconde
Robert the sonne of Willyā Slynger was bap: Nouember the vj$^{th}$
Joane the daughter of Robert Thompsonn was bap: Nouember the vj$^{th}$

Nomina defunctoru' eode' Anno.

Henry Laylande was buryed Januarie the iiij$^{th}$
Margret Wray was buryed Januarie the v$^{th}$

Nomina sponsaliu' eode' Anno.

Lawrence Lodge & Margret Tennante were marryed Januarie the xvij$^{th}$
Christofer Wade & Gennet Kydde were marryed Apryll the x$^{th}$

Nomina pueroru' baptizandoru' Anno Regni dominæ Reginæ Elizab: 23$^{tio}$

John the sonne of Richard Settle was baptized Nouember the xx$^{th}$
Symon the sonne of John Loftehouse was bap: Februarie the vj$^{th}$
Margret the daughter of Jeffray Costentyne was bap: Apryll the ix$^{th}$
Henry the sonne of Willya' Settle was bap: July the xxiij$^{th}$
Christofer the sonne of Richard Thompsonn was bap: August the vj$^{th}$
Frances the daughter of Henry Loynde was bap: August the xiij$^{th}$
Jone the daughter of Henry Garforth was bap: August the xiij$^{th}$
James the sonne of Anthonie Ward was bap: October the xv$^{th}$

Nomina defunctoru' eode' Anno.

Issabell Costentyne was buryed Nouember the xxiiij$^{th}$
Issabell Drake was buryed December the xviij$^{th}$
Willyã Laylande was buryed Februarie the xxiiij$^{th}$
Kateryne Kydde was buryed March the xiiij$^{th}$

Nomina sponsaliu' eode' Anno.

Christofer Hargraues & Margret Hyde were marryed Jaunarie the xvj$^{th}$
John Burtonn & Frances Pullayne were marryed Nouember the vj$^{th}$

Nomina pueroru' baptizand' Anno Regni Reginæ Elizabethæ 25$^{to}$

Lawrence the sonne of Robert Settle was baptized Nouember the xviij$^{th}$
Thomas the sonne of Myles Laylande was bap: Nouember the laste.

Nomina pueroru' baptizandoru' Anno salutis 1586 et Reginæ Eliz: 28$^{uo}$

Gennet the daughter of Willyã Todd was baptized Januarie the first.
Elizabeth the daughter of James Rayner was bap: March the x$^{th}$
Alice the daughter of Richard Settle was bap: Apryll the thirde.
Issabell the daughter of Richard Thompsonn was bap: June the fyrst.
Dyna the daughter of Anthonie Warde was bap: June the xij$^{th}$
John the sonne of Thomas Lambart was baptized October the ix$^{th}$
Hellen the daughter of Richard Layland was bap: December the xxviij$^{th}$
Oustos the sonne of Thomas Ayretonn was bap: Februarie the xx$^{th}$
Agnes the daughter of Thomas Wiggleswoorth was bap: March the xiiij$^{th}$

Nomina defunctoru' eode' Anno viz: Elizabethæ 28.

A mans childe of Thomas Ayretons was buryed the laste day of Januarie.
Alice Wiggleswoorth of Conistonn was buryed Apryll the xj$^{th}$
John Laylands wife was buryed Februarie the last.
Richard Todds wyfe was buryed Apryll the xxij$^{th}$

Nomina pueroru' baptiz eodem Anno.

Christofer the sonne of Willyã Broadbelt was baptized June the xxviiij$^{th}$

Nomina sponsaliu' eode' Anno.

Richard Pullayne & Margret Carlill were marryed October the iiij$^{th}$
Thomas Cocket & Issabell Costentyne were marryed October the ix$^{th}$
Thomas Wiggleswoorth & Mabell Clarke were marryed Januarie the xx$^{th}$

Nomina pueroru' baptiz: Anno domini 1587.

Christofer the sonne of Willya' Slinger was bap: Julye the xxiij$^{th}$
Alice the daughter of Robert Settle was bap: September the third.
Anthonie the sonne of Thomas Settle was bap: October the v$^{th}$

[A fol. 3. r.

Agnes the daughter of Thomas Blande was bap: Februrie the 26$^{th}$ eode' Anno.
Agnes the daughter of Robert Thompsonn was bap: Februarie the 28$^{th}$

Nomina sponsaliu' eode' anno.

Robert Wiggleswoorth & Gennet Laylande were marryed Januarie the 25th

Steauen Johnsonn & Hellen Lambarte were marryed Julye the 22th

Nomina defunctoru' eode' Anno.

Richard Wiggleswoorth was buryed in templo: the first of October.
Edward Hodgsonn was buryed December the vjth
Gennet Broadbelt wyddow was buryed Januarie the 22th
Gennet Ibbotsonn of Kylnsay was buryed Februarie the 22th

Nomina defunctoru' Anno domini 1588.

Thomas Hebden was buryed May the 24th
Myles Laylande was buryed June the 21th
A womans childe of Thomas Ayretons was buryed Julye the 22th
Agnes Francklande widdow was buryed September the 21th

nomina pueroru' baptiz: Anno domini 1589.

Jeane the daughter of Anthonie Ward was bap: March the ixth
Elizabeth the daughter of Willyā Todd was bap: March the xxth
Christofer the sonne of Richard Settle was bap: March the xxiiijth
Thomas the sonne of Richard Layland was bap: Apryll the 25th
Richard the sonn of Robert Wiggleswoorth was bap: May the 25th
Jeane the daughter of Richard Lambart was bap: June the 24th
Gennet the daughter of Thomas Wiggleswoorth was bap: September the 28th
Robert the sonne of Richard Pullain was bap: October the 26th
Christofer the sonne of Thomas Ayretonn was bap: Nouember the first
Elizabeth the daughter of Willya' Settle was bap: March the xxth
Thomas the sonne of Thomas Lambart was bap: May the fyrst.
Henry the sonne of John mydlā was bap: may the iijth
Agnes the daughter of Thomas Costentyne was bap: June the 24th

nomina defunctoru' eodem Anno.

Dina warde was buryed August the 12th giuen to the brydg one oke tree.
Agnes Franckland was buryed September the 18th
Margret Costentyne the wyfe of Henry Costentyne December the 15. giuen to the Chappell & brydge ijs

Nomina sponsaliu' Anno domini 1590.

Mathew walton & Issabell Battie were marryed Januarie the 28th
Robert wood & Gennet Parkinsonn were marryed Februarie the xjth

Nomina defunctoru' eode' Anno.

John Slinger Junior of Couishtonn was buryed Auguste the 30th
Kateryne Pickow was buried Februarie the 16th
Anne the wife of Richard Lambart was buryed March the 21th

nomina pueroru' baptizandoru' Anno domini 1591.

Lawrence the sonne of Thomas Settle was baptized August the 15th
John the base begotten sonne of Cicelie Graunge was bap: September the 12th

Elizabeth the daughter of Thomas Wiggleswoorth was bap: Nouember the 24th
Hellen the daughter of Anthonie warde was bap: Februarie the 20th
Dina the daughter of Richard Settle was bap: Februarie the 20th
Elizabeth also the daughter of the sayd Richard was bap: the same day.

nomina sponsaliu' code' anno vizt 1591.

Thomas Battie and Gennet Laylande were marryed Julie the third.

nomina defunctoru' code' anno.

Cicelie Graunge was buryed October the 12th
Thomas Ripplay of Conishtonn was buryed October the 13th
Elizabeth Francklande was buryed October the 22th

Nomina pueroru' baptiz: Anno 1592.

Anne the daughter of Richard Pullaine was baptized May the 8th
Jeane the daughter of Thomas Ayretonn was bap: Julye the 2th
Christofer the sonne of Thomas Lambart was bap: September the 28th
Arthur the sonne of Robert Settle was bap: nouember the 30th
Thomas wood the sonne of Roberte wood was bap: Januarie the vjth
George the sonne of Robert Wiggleswoorth was bap: Januarie the 20th
Roger the sonne of Robert Franckland was bap: Januarie the 20th

nomina sponsaliu' code' anno.

Henry Beecrofte & Elizabeth Hebden were marryed June the 12th
Thomas Tophan & Margrett Richardsonn were marryed Nouember the 20th

nomina defunctoru' code' Anno.

Gennet the daughter of George Horner was buryed September the 12th
Margret the wyfe of James Stapp was buryed October the 15th
Willyā the sonne of Richard Lambart was buryed Nouember the 29th
Edward Warde Warde was buryed December the 2th payde to the Chappell 3s 4d

Nomina pueroru' baptizandoru' Anno 1593.

Marie the daughter of Richard Lambart was bap: Februarie the 9th
Anthonie the sonne of Richard Pullayne was bap: March the 17th
Maude the daughter of Richard Settle was bap: October the 2d

Nomina sponsaliu' code' anno.

Thomas Skelding & Anne Blande were marryed May the 20th

Nomina pueroru' baptizandor' Anno 1594.

Helena Faldshay baptizata fuit primo die Januarij.
Margreta filia Thomæ Wiggleswoorth baptizata fuit Julij 21mo

[A fol. 3. v.

Anthonius filius Roberti Wiggleswoorth baptizatus fuit Augustij 18uo
Georgius filius Johannis Horner baptiz: fuit tercio die Decembris.
Petrus filius Roberti Woode baptiz: fuit Octobris 13cio die.

Nomina sponsaliu' eodem Anno.

Steauen Francklande & Elizabeth Settle were marryed June the 2$^{th}$
John Horner & Frances Battie were marryed June the 4$^{th}$

Nomina defunctoru' eode' Anno.

Georgius filius Roberti Wiggleswoorth sepultus fuit Julij 25$^{to}$
Anthonius filius Roberti Wiggleswoorth sepultus fuit Augustij 22$^{do}$
Thomas Warde filius Anthonij Ward sepultus fuit Septembris 27$^{mo}$
Geneta Kydd sepulta fuit Decembris 5$^{to}$ die.

Nomina pueroru' baptizandoru' Anno domini 1595$^{to}$

Thomas Hebden filius Johannis Hebden bap: fuit Decembris 3$^{o}$ die.
Elizabetha Franckland baptizata fuit vltimo die Februarij.

Nomina defunctoru' eode' anno.

Thomas Lambarte filius Thomæ Lambart sepultus fuit Marcij 24$^{to}$

Nomina pueroru' baptizandoru' Anno 1596.

Franciscus Lambart filius Richardi baptizatus fuit primo die Maij.
Lawrencius Costentyne filius Thomæ bap: fuit Maij 29$^{no}$
Richardus filius Thomæ Ayretonn bap: fuit Februarij 27$^{mo}$

Nomina sponsaliu Anno predicto.

Lawrence Laylande & Hellen Battie Nouember the 23$^{th}$

Nomina defunctoru' eode' Anno.

Franciscus filius Richardi Lambart sepultus fuit vltimo die Julij.
Agneta filia Thomæ Costentyne sepulta fuit Augustij sexto die.
vxor Roberti Pullaine sepulta fuit Augustij 28$^{uo}$ die.
vxor Jacobi Parkinsonn sepulta fuit februarij 5$^{to}$ die.

Nomina pueroru' bap: Anno domini 1597.

Richardus Wiggleswoorth filius Thomæ baptiz: fuit 3$^{cio}$ die Aprilis.
Anna Lambart filia Richardi bap: fuit 10$^{mo}$ die Aprilis.
Gracia Layland filia Lawrencij bap: fuit 28$^{uo}$ die Augustij.
Isabella filia Johannis Horner bap: fuit 28$^{uo}$ die Octobris.
Richardus filius Roberti Faldshay bap: fuit 10$^{mo}$ die Februarij.

Nomina' defunctoru' eode' Anno.

Simonus Lofthous fuit sepultus 4$^{to}$ die Maij.
Johannes Pearsonn fuit sepultus 13$^{o}$ die Maij.
Thomas Settle sepultus fuit 15$^{to}$ die Maij.
Galfridus Costentyne sepultus fuit 22$^{do}$ die Maij.
Genneta vxor Christoferi Wade sepul fuit p$^{r}$imo Junij. payd to y$^{e}$ Chappell iij$^{s}$
Elizabetha vxor Jacobi Rayner sepulta fuit 10$^{mo}$ die Maij.
Gracia Tennante vxor Johannis sepulta fuit 19$^{no}$ die Junij. payd to y$^{e}$ Chappell iij$^{s}$ 4$^{d}$
Geneta Battie sepulta fuit 5$^{to}$ die Julij.
Robertus Settle fuit sepultus 22$^{do}$ die Julij.
Elizabetha Ibbotsonn vxor Thomæ fuit sepulta 23$^{o}$ die Julij.
Richardus filius Thomæ Wiggleswoorth sepult: fuit 30$^{mo}$ die Julij.
Rogerus filius Georgij Horner sepultus fuit 2$^{do}$ die Augustij.

Alicia Franckland sepulta fuit 2do die Septembris.
Genneta vxor Richardi Settle sepulta fuit vltimo die Octobris.
Alicia Pearsonn sepulta fuit vltimo die Octobris.

Nomina pueroru' baptizandoru' Anno domini 1598.

Issabell Wiggleswoorth filia Thomæ baptizata fuit sexto die Augustij.
Susanna Lambart filia Richardi bap: fuit 18uo die Octobris.
Maria Battie filia Johannis baptiz: fuit 3o die decembris.
Anthonius Ward filius Eduardi bap: fuit secundo die Februarij.
Elizabetha Hebden filia Johannis bap: fuit 21mo die Februarij.
Genneta filia xpopheri' Ibbotsonn bap: fuit 17mo die marcij.
Issabela Franckland filia Roberti bap: fuit 18uo die Marcij.

Nomina defunctoru' eodem Anno.

Richard Faldshay the sonne of Robert was buryed June 20th
Isabell the daughter of Willyã Broadbelt was buryed Julie 27th
Frances Horner the wyfe of John Horner was buryed August the 8th
The wyfe of John Pearsonn was buryed September the 15th
Agnes Settle the daughter of Christofer was buryed Februari the 7th
The wyfe of Willyã Lambart was buryed Februarie the 17th

nomina pueroru' baptizdoru' Anno domini 1599.

fili Roberti Wigglesworth baptiz: fuit August the xiiijth
John Ibbotsonn the sonne of Christofer was bap: October the 23th
Edwardus hartlay filius Lawrencij baptiz: October the 26th

nomina sponsaliu' Anno domini 1599.

John Horner & Gennet Tennant were marryed the last of September.
Willyã Inman & Margret Costentyne were marryed October ye 7th
James Tennant & Margret Battie were marryed Nouember the 18th

nomina defunctoru' eode' anno. [A fol. 4. r.

Willyã Lambart was buryed Nouember the 21th
Thomas Ibbotsonn was buryed Januarie the xiijth

Nomina pueroru' baptizand Anno 1600.

Elizabetha Harner filia Johannis baptiz: fuit Junij 16to
Elizabetha filia Jacobi Tennant baptiz: fuit Septembris 7mo die.
Alicia filia Richardi Lambart baptiz: fuit primo die Nouembris.
Wilhelmus Ayretonn filius Thomæ bap: fuit 14to die Januarij.

nomina defunctoru' eode' anno.

Susanna Lambart filia Richardi sepulta fuit 6to die Aprilis.
Christoferus Lambart sepultus fuit 2do die Januarij.
Agneta Hodgsonn sepulta fuit 21mo die Junij.
Henricus Settle filius Roberti sepultus fuit 27mo die Junij.
Cicelia vxor Thomæ Bland sepulta fuit Junij 29 die.
Hellena vxor Wil'mi Broadbelt sepulta fuit 4to die Januarij.

Nomina sponsaliu' eode' anno.

Edward Hebden & Margret waylock were marryed Januarie the 27th

Nomina pueroru' bap: Anno domini 1601.

Hellen the daughter of John Battie was bap: June the 28th
Alice the daughter of Thomas Wiggleswoorth was bap: August ye 9th

George the sonn of Henry Bland was bap: the 23$^{th}$ day of August.
John the sonne of Lawrence Hartlay was bap: August the 30$^{th}$
John the sonne of Richard Battie was bap: September the first
Jone the daughter of Edward Hebden was bap: October the 2j$^{th}$
James the sonne of xpopher Ibbotsonn was bap: Nouember the 8$^{th}$
Thomas the sonne of Edward Warde was bap: Nouember the xv$^{th}$
Robert the sonne of Lawrence Layland the xv$^{th}$ of Nouember.
Elizabeth the daughter of Christofer Drake was bap: Nouember the xxj$^{th}$
John the sonne of Richard Tennant was bap: Januari the xvij$^{th}$

Nomina sponsaliu' anno eode'.

John Bawdwayne and Gennet Kydd were marryed September y$^{e}$ xxj$^{th}$
Thomas Blande and Margret Knowles were marryed September y$^{e}$ 27$^{th}$
John Jacksonn and Jeane Settle were marryed Nouember the 18$^{th}$

Nomina defunctoru' eode' Anno.

Elizabeth the daughter of Willyā Settle was buryed August the x$^{th}$
George the sonne of Henry Blande was buryed September the viij$^{th}$
Elizabeth Hebden was buryed Januarie the xv$^{th}$

Nomina pueroru' bap: Anno domini 1602.

Agnes the daughter of John Horner was bap: May the fyrst.
Edmund the sonne of Robert Faldshay was bap: June the xiij$^{th}$
Thomas the sonne of Robert Franckland was bap: Julie the xxvij$^{th}$
John the sonne of James Tennant was bap: Nouember the xiij$^{th}$
Issabell the daughter of Richard Lambart was bap: the xiiij$^{th}$ of Nouember.
John & Francis sonns of Edward Hebden were bap: March the syxt.

nomina sponsaliu' anno p$^{r}$dicto.

Willyā Howsonn & Margret Boultonn were marryed Apryll the 19$^{th}$
Richard Costentyne & Agnes Hebden were marryed June the xj$^{th}$

Nomina defunctoru' Anno p$^{r}$dicto.

Elizabeth Wigglesworth sepulta fuit quarto die Junij.
John Layland was buryed the xxj$^{th}$ day of Julie.
George Horner was buryed the xxix day of Auguste.
Gennet the daughter of Thomas Settle was buryed Nouember the xj$^{th}$

Nomina pueroru' bap: Anno 1603.

Anne the daughter of John Hebden was baptized Februarie the xiij$^{th}$
Agnes the daughter of Richard Battie was baptized Feb the xv$^{th}$
Anne the daughter of John Settle March the 20$^{th}$
Richard the sonne of Richard Tennante December the x$^{th}$

Nomina defunctoru' eode' anno.

John the sonne of James Tennante was buryed.
Anne Laylande widdow was buried Nouember the xxv$^{th}$
Hellen the wyfe of Anthony Ward was buried the xxix$^{th}$ of Nouember. payd to the Church iij$^{s}$ iiij$^{d}$

Nomina puerorū baptizandorū Anno domini 1604.

Willyam the sonne of James Tennant Aprill the viij$^{th}$
Hellen the daughter of John Jacksonn May the vj$^{th}$
Alice the daughter of Edmund Richardsonn Julie the xv$^{th}$
Margret the daughter of Christofer Drake June the last.
Elizabeth the base begotten daughter of Agnes Costentyne September ix$^{th}$
Gennet the daughter of John Horner was bap: September the xxij$^{th}$
Willyā the sonne of Richard Lambart September the xxiij$^{th}$
Anne the daughter of Robert faldshay Nouember the first.
Agnes the daughter of Lawrence Hartlay December the second.
Henry the sonne of Thomas Ayretonn Januarie the 6$^{th}$
Alice the daughter of Lawrence Layland Januarie the ......
Jeane the base begotten daughter of Elizabeth Hodgsonn Februarie the x$^{th}$

Nomina sponsaliū Anno domini 1604. [A fol. 4. v.

Thomas Broadbelt & Frances Wilkinsonn were marryed Nouember y$^{e}$ 4$^{th}$

nomina defunctorū eodē anno.

Agnes the wyfe of Richard Costentyne was buryed march the 20$^{th}$
Jeane Costentyne widdow was buryed Apryll the 21$^{th}$
An Infant the sonne of Thomas Wiggleswoorth was buryed August 19$^{th}$
Agnes the daughter of Jefray Costentyne was buryed September y$^{e}$ xj$^{th}$
Gennet the wyfe of John Horner was buryed September the xvij$^{th}$
Grace the wyfe of John Hodgsonn was buryed Nouember the xiiij$^{th}$
Gennet the daughter of John Horner was buryed September y$^{e}$ 18$^{th}$
Gennet the daughter of Willyā Broadbelt was buried Februarie y$^{e}$ 18$^{th}$

Nomina sponsaliū Anno domini 1605.

Robert Stockdayle & Hellen Winterburne June the seconde.

Nomina puerorū baptiz: eodē anno.

Anne the daughter of John Jacksonn was bap: August the 4$^{th}$
Robert the sonne of Thomas Wiggleswoorth was bap: August the 20$^{th}$
Gennet the daughter of Richard Battie was bap: September y$^{e}$ 29$^{th}$
Anne the daughter of xpofer Ibbotsonn was bap: Nouember the 17$^{th}$
John the sonne of Richard Costentyne was bap: March the seconde.
Alice the daughter of Thomas Broadbelt was bap: March the seconde.

Nomina defunctorū eodē anno.

Agnes the daughter of Lawrence Hartlay Apryll the fyrst.
John Hebdenn of Conishtonn Apryll the fourth.
Anthony Woode of Northcoate June y$^{e}$ 29$^{th}$ payd to the Chappell 3$^{s}$ 4$^{d}$
Katheryne Hebden August the fyrst.
Lawrence Hartlay August the vij$^{th}$
John Hodgsonn August the xiiij$^{th}$
Grace the wyfe of Lawrence Hartlay September.
Thomas Ayretonn of Scarthcoate Nouember the xij$^{th}$
Agnes the wyfe of John Battie of Conishtonn Nouember the xviij$^{th}$

Margret the daughter of Richard Layland of Chappelhouse Januarie y^e^ x^th^
Agnes the daughter of Richard Battie March the ......
Alice the daughter of Thomas Broadbelt March the xij^th^
John the sonne of Richard Costentyne March the xvj^th^
Alice the daughter of Lawrence Laylande March the xv.

Nomina sponsaliu' Anno domini 1606.

Henry Thompsonn & Gennet Winterburne were marryed may the xj^th^
Thomas Battie & Agnes Wiggleswoorth were marryed June the fift.
Richard Todde & Hellen Laylande were marryed July the vj^th^
Willyã Stockdayle & Margret Lambart August the third.
Richard Todd & Susan Fauell August the xix^th^
George Smyth & Margret Skelding Nouember the seconde.
Robert Martonn & Agnes Fawcett Februarie the sixth.

Nomina pueroru' bap: code' anno.

Richard the sonne of Robert Franckland was bap: Apryll the vj^th^
Leonard the sonne of Edward Hebden was bap: Julie the vj^th^
Agnes the daughter of James Tennant was bap: October the xij^th^
Roberte the sonne of John Settle was bap: October the xxj^th^
Elizabeth the daughter of Edmund Richardsonn Januarie the iiij^th^
Christofer the sonne of Henry Thompsonn was bap: Januarie the xvj^th^
Issabell the daughter of Lawrence Layland was bap: Januarie the xviij^th^

Nomina defunctoru' code' anno.

Anne the daughter of Richard Tennant was buryed Apryll y^e^ xxix^th^
Margret the wyfe of John Tennant was buryed May the 24^th^ in temp.
Robert the sonne of John Settle was buryed October the 22^th^
Issabell the wyfe of xpopher Settle was buryed Nouember the last.
Gennet the wife of Thomas Ripplay was buried December the fyrst.
An Infante the daughter of Rycharde Todd was buryed Januarie the thirde.

Nomina sponsaliu' Anno domini 1607.

Willyã Sydgsweeke & Grace Ibbotsonn Aprill the xxvj^th^
Robert Slynger & Margret Layland June the xxj^th^
Robert Ripplay als. Clarke & Margret Snell June the laste.
Thomas Tennante & Anne Tennant Nouember the last.
M^d^ that Roger Touler Churchwarden Anno 1605 had & Receiued of George Warde for his fathers buryall in the Chappell 3^s^ 4^d^ w^ch^ hee also payde vnto Thomas Battie Churchwarden in Anno 1606 in the ...sence of vs Henry Ibbotsonn Richard Costentyne & others.

Nomina pueroru' bap: Anno domini 1607.

Elizabeth the daughter of Richard Costentyne May the fyrst.
Issabell the daughter of John Battie of Kylnsay May the xiiij^th^
Richard the sonn of John Jacksonn May the xxiiij^th^
Anne the daughter of John Garforth May the xxiiij^th^

nomina pueroru' baptiz: anno code'. [A fol. 5. r.

Willyã the sonne of Richard Todde was bap: Nouember the xxj^th^
Roberte the sonne of Willyã Sydgsweeke Januarie the last.

Thomas the sonne of Thomas Battie (late deceased) Januarie the last.
Willyā the sonne of Robert Slinger March the xx^th^
Anne the daughter of Christopher Drake the sayd xx^th^ of March.

Nomina defunctoru' eode' anno.

Thomas Battie of Conishtonn was buryed August the x^th^
Willyā the sonne of Richard Todd was buryed Nouember the xxij^th^
Thomas Drake was buryed Januarie the xij^th^

Nomina sponsaliu' Anno domini 1608.

John Willsonn & Anne Hebden September the xj^th^
Richard Lightfoote & Elizabeth Costentyne Januarie the 24^th^

nomina pueroru' baptiz anno p^r^dicto.

Hellen the daughter of Edwarde warde was bap: Apryll the seconde.
Agnes the daughter of Richard Lambert was bap: September y^e^ vj^th^
Robert the sonne of Richard Battie was bap: October the xxx^th^
Richard the sonne of Richard Todde was bap: Nouember the xix^th^
Willyā the sonne of Richard Tennant was bap: Januarie the fyrst.
Thomas the sonne of Robert Ripplay was bap: Januarie the fyrst.
Anne the daughter of Edward Hebden was bap: Januarie the syxt.
Henry the sonne of John Garforth was bap: Januarie the xx^th^
Gennet the daughter of James Tennante Februarie the seconde.
George the sonne of xpofer Ibbotsonn was bap: Februarie the xix^th^

Nomina defunctoru' eode' anno.

Thomas Touler was buried the xix day of June.
Katheryne Layland was buryed Nouember the x^th^
Dorethie Markendayle was buried Januarie the xvij^th^
Henry the sonne of John Garforth was buryed Februarie the xxij^th^
Henry Costentyne of Conishtonn was buryed March the xv^th^

Nomina sponsaliu' Anno domini 1609.

Richard Costentyne & Issabell Settle were marryed June the xxij^th^
George Tennante & Margret Smyth were marryed June the xxiij^th^
Willyā Layland & Gennet Battie were marryed Julie the ix^th^

nomina pueroru' baptizandoru' eode' anno.

Thomas the sonne of John Settle was bap: June the 30^th^
Richard Willsonn the sonne of John was bap: July the xxiij^th^
John Willsonn the sonne of the sayde John was bap: the sayd xxiij^th^ of Julie.
Jeane the daughter of Edmund Richardsonn was bap: September the x^th^
Henry Costentyne the sonne of Richard was bap: Januarie the vij^th^
John Sydgsweck sonne of Willyā was bap: Januarie the xx^th^
Henry the sonne of Lawrence Layland was bap: Januarie the xxj^th^

Nomina defunctoru' eode' anno.

George Laylande was buryed March the xxvj^th^
Alice Winterburne was buryed Apryll the xiij^th^
Richard Willsonn the sonne of John was buryed August (?) viij^th^
Willyā Todd was buryed September the ......

xpopher the sonne of Willyã Slinger was buryed October the xix^th^
Edmunde Richardsonn was buryed Nouember the vij^th^
Jeane the daughter of the sayde Edmund was buryed Nouember the vij^th^
Agnes the wyfe of Robert Martonn was buryed Nouember the xix^th^
Issabell Battie widdow was buryed Februarie the vij^th^
James Stapper was buryed Februarie the xviij^th^ payd for his graue 3^s^ 4^d^ to Edward Warde & Willyã Layland Churchwardens for the yeare aboue wrytten.

Nomina sponsaliu' Anno domini 1610.

John Settle and Anne Ham'ertonn were marryed August the xx^th^

Nomina pueroru' baptizandoru' eodem Anno.

Edward the sonne of John Battie was bap: Apryll the xv^th^
John the sonne of George Tennant was bap: Apryll the xvij^th^
Elizabeth the base begotten daughter of Issabell Thompsonn was bap: May the xx^th^
Margret the daughter of John Jacksonn was bap: June the xvij^th^
John the sonne of Henry Thompsonn was bap: July the fyrst.
Alice the daughter of the sayde Henry bap: the same day.
Anne the daughter of Edward warde was bap: August the xvij^th^
John the sonne of Willyã Laylande was bap: December the vij^th^
Robert Costentyne the sonne of Richard Costentyne Junior bap: December the xx^th^
John the sonn of Richard Lambart December the xxvj^th^

Nomina defunctoru' eode' anno.

Christofer Settle was buryed May the xvj^th^
Robert Ibbotsonn of Kylnsay was buryed Januarie the vj^th^
Francis Marscue was buryed Februarie the iiij^th^
Robert Ripplay was buryed Februarie the xxvj^th^
Elizabeth tennant the seruante of John Tennant was buryed March the seconde

Nomina sponsaliu' Anno domini 1610. [A fol. 5. v.

Robert Costentyne and Agnes Battie were marryed October the vij^th^
Robert Goodfellow & Margret Brayshaw were marryed Nouember the xix^th^

nomina pueroru' bap: eode' anno.

Robert the sonn of John Settle was bap: March the 19^th^

Nomina sponsaliu' Anno domini 1611.

Henry Buckle & Agnes Weste were marryed Apryll the viij^th^
Richard Walker and Hellen Settle were marryed Apryll the xxiiij^th^
Willyã Tophan & Hellen Warde were marryed Nouember the xviij^th^

Nomina pueroru' baptizandoru' eode' anno.

Margret the daughter of Richard Todd was bap: Apryll the xxj^th^
Richard the sonne of Robert Costentyne July the xvj^th^
Elizabeth the daughter of Henry Ibbotsonn was bap: October the xviij^th^

Richard the sonne of John Settle of Kylnsay was bap : Januarie the vij$^{th}$
Margret the daughter of Richard Battie March xiij$^{th}$

Nomina sponsaliu' Anno domini 1612.

Richard Broadbelt & Dorethie Layland were marryed Julye the seconde.

nomina pueroru' bap : eode' Anno.

Isabell the daughter of James Tennant May the vij$^{th}$
Margret the daughter of Robert Francklande May the last.
Richard the sonne of Richard Costentyne July the xix$^{th}$
Alice the daughter of Robert Slinger August the xvj$^{th}$
Margret the daughter of Lawrence Laylande September the viij$^{th}$
Margret the daughter of Henry Ibbotsonn October the xviij$^{th}$
Richard the sonne of Henry Thompsonn Nouember the xxiiij$^{th}$
Margret the daughter of Willyā Sydgsweeke December the iiij$^{th}$
Margret the daughter of John Battie of Kylnsay Januarie the xxij$^{th}$
Anne the daughter of John Settle of Conishtonn Februarie the xxiiij$^{th}$
Sarye (?) Willsonn the daughter of John March the vij$^{th}$

Nomina defunctoru' eode' anno.

Thomas Hodgsonn of Scarthcoate was buryed July the v$^{th}$
Margret Skott als Willsonn was buryed July the xxij$^{th}$
Margret the wyfe of Thomas Hodgsonn was buryed July the xxij$^{th}$
Gennet the wyfe Henry Thompsonn was buryed Nouember the 24$^{th}$
Richard the sonne of Richard Costentyne senior was buryed December y$^{e}$ 21$^{th}$

Nomina sponsaliu' Anno domini 1613.

Willyā Atkinsonn & Issabell Knowles were marryed the x$^{th}$ of May.
Willyā Taytham & Hellen Costentyne were marryed May the xxij$^{th}$
Christofer Hogge & Jeane Warde were marryed Januarie the xxvij$^{th}$

Nomina pueroru' bap : eode' anno.

Hellen the daughter of Richard Broadbelt was bap : May the xxj$^{th}$
Willyā the sonne of Richard Todd was bap : Nouember the xvij$^{th}$
Elizabeth the daughter of John Settle of Northcoat Nouember the xxj$^{th}$
Issabell the daughter of Richard Costentyne Junior Januarie the xxx$^{th}$

Nomina defunctoru' eode' anno.

Henry Settle was buryed May the xx$^{th}$
James Slinger was buryed the xxviij$^{th}$ of May. payd 3$^{s}$ 4$^{d}$ his gyft.
Arthur Wade was buryed October the xxvj$^{th}$
An Infante the sonne of Richard Costentyne senior was buryed october y$^{e}$ last.
Willyā Settle of Kylnsay was buryed the xxix$^{th}$ day of Nouember.
Anne the daughter of one John Graues was buried December the xxvj$^{th}$

Nomina sponsaliu' Anno domini 1614.

Raphe Settle & Susann Touler were marryed May the xxx$^{th}$
Richard Hine & Elizabeth Franckland were marryed Februarie y$^{e}$ xij$^{th}$

Nomina pueroru' baptiz : eode anno.

Issabell the daughter of John Graues was bap : Apryll the third.
Henry the sonne of Robert Costentyne was bap : Apryll the tenth.

Christofer the sonne of John Settle was bap: Apryll the xxiiij[th]
Margret the daughter of Raphe Settle was bap: August the vij[th]
Elizabeth the supposed daughter of one John Lodge October the seconde.
Margret the daughter of Willyã Layland was bap: October the xvj[th]
Thomas the sonne of Richard Battie was bap: Februarie the xix[th]

Nomina defunctoru' eode' anno.

Christofer Ayretonn was buryed Apryll the xv[th]
Willyã Atchinsonn was buryed May the xix[th]
A poore Childe called John Madisson was buryed June the xvj[th]
Roger Touler was buryed October the seconde.
Anne Ibbotsonn was buryed December the iiij[th]

Nomina sponsaliu' Anno domini 1615.

Anthonie Spurret & Jeane Crauen were marryed May the iiij[th]
Richard Laylande and Alice Atchinsonn were marryed May the xxx[th]

Nomina pueroru' bap: eode' anno.

Margret the daughter of Richard Costentyne senior was bap: Apryll the vij[th]
Grace the daughter of John Settle was bap: Apryll the xxiij[th]

nomina bap: anno predicto vizt 1615. [A fol. 6. r.

Anne the daughter of Henry Ibbotsonn was bap: August the thirde.
Elizabeth the daughter of Willyã Sydgsweeke was bap: october y[e] x[th]
Anne the daughter of Lawrence Settle was bap: Nouember y[e] viij[th]
Edward the sonne of Richard Broadbelt was bap: Januarie xviij[th]
Richard the sonne of Lawrence Layland was bap: March the ix[th]

Nomina defunctoru' eode' Anno.

Gennet the wyfe of Thomas Battie was buryed May the vj[th]
Thomas Battie was buryed June the xj[th]
Gennet Caluard was buryed March the xxiij[th]

Nomina sponsaliu' Anno 1616.

John Wiggleswoorth & Hellen Breaks were marryed Apryll the first.
Lawrence Costentyne & Jeane Ayretonn were marryed June the xix[th]

Nomina pueroru' baptiz: eode' anno.

Edwarde the sonne of Edwarde Warde was bap: Apryll the xxj[th]
Elizabeth the daughter of one George Nutter was bap: May the v[th]
Gennet the daughter of Anthonie Couch was bap: June the xiij[th]
Robert the sonne of Roger Francklande was bap: Februarie the ij[th]
Margret the daughter of Robert Costentyne was Februarie the iiij[th]

Nomina defunctoru' eode' anno.

Agnes the wife of George Horner was buryed May the xxvj[th]

Nomina sponsaliu' Anno domini 1617.

Henry Snell & Alice Richardsonn were marryed the xxviij day of June.
Thomas Kydd & Issabell Luptonn were Marryed.

Nomina puerorū' bap: Anno p'dicto.

Arthur the sonne of Christofer Wade was bap: May the viij^th^
Elizabeth the daughter of George Tennant was bap: May the vij^th^
Mary the daughter of Henry Ibbotsonn was bap: July the seconde.
Peter the base borne childe of Elizabeth Wiggleswoorths was bap: July y^e^ xj^th^
James the sonne of James Rayner was bap: August the laste.
Gennet the daughter of Richard Costentyne senior was bap: October the v^th^
Thomas the sonne of Richard Todd was bap: December the xvij^th^
Richard the sonne of John Settle of Conishtonn was bap: March the viij^th^
John the sonne of Robert Costentyne of Conishtonn was bap: March the xj^th^

Nomina defunctorū' eode' Anno.

Margret the daughter of Robert Costentyne was buryed March the 25^th^
Alice the wyfe of Christopher Drake was buryed August the xxij^th^
Thomas Costentyne of Kylnsay was buryed the xij^th^ Januarie.
Issabell Layland was buryed Februarie the ix^th^
M^d^ that Richard Pullaine payd to the paynter ix^s^ John Layland payd to the same vj^s^ besyds James Francklands gifte so also imployed.

nomina sponsaliū' Anno domini 1618.

John Layland & Alice West were marryed Apryll the xv^th^
Willyā Tennante & Margret Knowles were marryed July the vj^th^
Thomas Broadlay & Hellen Layland were married Nouember the xxv^th^
Symon Willkinsonn & Margerie Procter were marryed december y^e^ viij^th^
Bartholomew Armisteade & Anne Pullaine were marryed December y^e^ ix^th^

Nomina puerorū' baptiz: eode' Anno.

Issabell the daughter of Lawrence Costentyne was bap: May y^e^ vj^th^
Willyā the sonne of Richard Broadbelt was bap: Julie the xv^th^
John the sonne of John Laylande was bap: December the xxv^th^
Anthonie the sonne of Willyā Sydgsweek was bap: Januarie the xxiiij^th^
Elizabeth the daughter of Roger Franckland was bap: Februarie y^e^ xx^th^
Alice the daughter of John Settle of Conishtonn March the xxij^th^

Nomina defunctorū' eode' anno.

Richard the sonne of John Settle of Conishtonn was buryed Apryll the xix^th^
Arthur the sonne of Christopher Wade was buryed May the iiij^th^
Richard the sonne of Lawrence Layland May the xxj^th^
John Jacksonn of Kylnsay was buryed October the xiij^th^
Thomas Wiggleswoorth of Conishtonn was buryed Januarie the xx^th^
Grace the daughter of John Settle was buryed Januarie y^e^ last.
An Infant the daughter of Richard Battie was buryed Februarie the thirde.

Grace the wyfe of Richard Battie was buryed Februrarie the vj$^{th}$
Henry Garforth of Kylnsay Junior was buryed March the xvj$^{th}$
Alice the daughter of John Settle was buryed March the xix$^{th}$

Nomina pueroru' baptizandoru' Anno domini 1619.

Elizabeth the daughter of Lawrence Layland was bap: October the xxiiij$^{th}$
Cutbart the sonne of Christofer Wade was bap: Nouember the xvij$^{th}$

Nomina defunctoru' anno p'dicto.

Elizabeth Tennant widdow was buryed Apryll the xij$^{th}$
Thomas the sonne of xpopher Audersonn was buryed Apryll the xix$^{th}$
John Fauell was buryed August the xxij$^{th}$
Elizabeth the daughter of George Tennante December the xix$^{th}$
Anthonie the sonne of Willyā Sydgsweeke Februarie the ......
Thomas the sonne of Lawrence Layland March the xvj$^{th}$

Nomina pueroru' baptizandoru' Anno domini 1620. [A fol. 6. v.

Thomas the sonne of Henry Ibbotsonn was bap: Apryll the ix$^{th}$
Richard the sonne of Richard Fyrth was bap: May the xxiiij$^{th}$
Richard the sonne of John Layland was bap: Februarie seconde.
Issabel the daughter of Christofer Aldersonn Februarie y$^{e}$ xj$^{th}$
Elizabeth the daughter of Lawrence Costentyne August y$^{e}$ viij$^{th}$

Nomina defuctoru' eode' Anno.

Thomas Skelding was buryed Apryll the xiij$^{th}$
Richard Thompsonn was buryed Apryll the xxvj$^{th}$
Thomas the sonne of Henry Ibbotsonn was buryed May y$^{e}$ xx$^{th}$
Anne the wyfe of Thomas Skelding was buryed December x$^{th}$
An infant the sonne of Willyā Sydgsweek was buryed Februarie y$^{e}$ x$^{th}$
Thomas Costentyne of Conishtonn was buryed Februarie y$^{e}$ xxj$^{th}$
Richard the sonne of John Layland was buryed Februarie y$^{e}$ 23$^{th}$

Nomina pueroru' baptizandoru' Anno domini 1621.

Elizabeth the daughter of Chrystofer Wayde was bap: May the 13$^{th}$
Dorethie the daughter of Roger Franckland was bap: Julie the xv$^{th}$
Thomas the sonne of Henry Ibbotsonn was bap: August the xij$^{th}$
Margret y$^{e}$ daughter of Thomas Settle was bap: August the xix$^{th}$

Nomina defunctoru' eode' anno.

Willyā Broadbelt was buryed May the xvj$^{th}$
Robert the sonne of Robert Costentyne was buryed June the xviij$^{th}$
Thomas Lambart of Kylnsay was buryed June the xx$^{th}$
Richard Settle of Kylnsay was buryed Nouember the xvij$^{th}$
Henry Garforth senior was buryed Nouember the xxv$^{th}$
Receiued by Richard Costentyne & Richard Ayretonn churchwardens 3$^{s}$ 4$^{d}$
John Parrot was buryed December the seconde.
Elizabeth Hebden was buryed December the xxx$^{th}$
Roger Franckland was buryed Januarie the xxj$^{th}$
James Franckland was buryed Februarie y$^{e}$ 5$^{th}$ dedit capellæ 5$^{s}$
Margret the wyfe of Roger Touler was buryed Februarie the 5$^{th}$

Nomina pueroru' baptizandoru' Anno domini 1622.

Agnes the daughter of George Tennant was bap: March the laste.
Willyā the sonne of John Layland was bap: Apryll the fyrst.
Anne the daughter of Christofer Wad was bap: June the xvjth
Issabell the daughter of Robert Costentyne was bap: June the xxiijth
John the sonne of Thomas Layland was bap: July the xxixth
George the sonne of Anthonie Warde was bap: October the vjth

Nomina defunctoru' eode' Anno.

John the sonne of Thomas Layland was buryed August the xjth
James West was buryed August the xvijth
George the sonne of Anthonie Warde was buryed October the xxjth
Margret Costentyne widdow was buryed October the xxiiijth
Richard Fawcet a straunger was buryed Nouember the xxijth
Md that John Layland Churchwarden in anno 1623 had & Received 5s from the hands of James Tennant of Conishtonn wch was the gyfte of James Franckland deceassed & by John Layland payd ouer to one Willsonn a paynter for pte of his composition for the Chappell.

Nomina pueroru' baptizandoru' Anno domini 1623.

Hellen the daughter of Thomas Settle was bap: September the xiiijth
Anthonie the sonne of Henry Ibbotsonn was bap: Januarie the xjth
Elizabeth the daughter of Thomas Layland was bap: Februarie ye xxijth

Nomina defunctoru' anno prdicto.

Elizabeth the wyfe of Arthur Wade was buryed July the ixth
James Rayner was buryed July the first his gifte to the Chappell xxd payde to Richard Costentyne & Richard Ayretonn Churchwardens 1624.
Anne the daughter of Christofer Wade was buryed August the viijth
Thomas Allen a stranger was buryed Nouember the xxiijth

Nomina sponsaliu' Anno domini 1624.

George Horner & Anne Hebden were marryed June the vijth
Anthony Winterburne & Mary Lambart were marryed December ye xvjth
Christofer Curteous & Elizabeth Furnace were marryed Januarie ye xiijth
Edmunde Horseman & Hellen Stonay were marryed Januarie ye xxijth
James Coate & Anne Lambart were marryed Februarie ye second.

Nomina pueroru' baptiz: eode' anno.

Mathew the sonne of John Settle was bap: Aprill the iiijth
Margret the daughter of Christofer Wade was bap: Apryll the iiijth
Thomas the sonne of Lawrence Costentyne bap: Aprill the xjth
John the sonne of Roger Franckland bap: Aprill the xviijth

nomina pueroru' bap: Anno prdicto. [A fol. 7. r.

Thomas the sonne of Anthonie Ward was bap: June the xxth
Augustine the sonne of Roger Stonay was bap: September the ixth
Christofer the sonne of Willyā Sydgsweeke was bap: September xixth

Nomina defunctoru' eodem anno.

Willyā Layland of Conishtonn was buryed Apryll the xv$^{th}$
Robert Martonn of Conishtonn was buryed June the xv$^{th}$
Thomas the sonne of Anthonie Warde was buryed July the xx$^{th}$
Mathew the sonne of John Settle was buryed March the xxiij$^{th}$

Nomina sponsaliu' Anno domini 1625.

Richard Costentyne & Margret Wiggleswoorth were marryed June y$^{e}$ xvj$^{th}$
John Bucktrout & Grace Tennant were Marryed Julie the vij$^{th}$
Thomas Hebden & Elizabeth Tennant were marryed Julie the x$^{th}$

nomina pueroru' bap : eode' anno.

Jeane the daughter of Willyā Atkinsonn and Lyttonn was bap : March y$^{e}$ xxv$^{th}$
Margret the daughter of Anthonie Warde was bap : Julie the xx$^{th}$
Grace the daughter of John Battie was bap : August the vij$^{th}$
Gennet the daughter of John Layland was bap : September the xviij$^{th}$
John the sonne of George Horner was bap : September the xxj$^{th}$
Margret the daughter of Robert Costentyne was bap : Nouember xxvj$^{th}$
Issabell the daughter of Richard Ayretonn was bap : December y$^{e}$ xiiij$^{th}$
Richard the sonne of Roger Francklande was bap : Februarie the v$^{th}$
Henry the sonne of Henry Ibbotsonn was bap : Februarie the xix$^{th}$

Nomina defunctoru' eode' Anno.

John the sonne of Roger Franckland was buryed Apryll the vij$^{th}$
Margret the daughter of Christofer Wade was buryed June the seconde.
Gennet the wyfe of Francis Garforth was buryed September the xix$^{th}$
John the sonne of George Horner was buryed Nouember the xiiij$^{th}$
Md that Anthony Warde did pay vnto Richard Costentyne & Richard Ayretonn Churchwardens in Anno 1624 vj$^{s}$ viij$^{d}$ for the buryall of his 2 Children in the Chappell.

Nomina sponsaliu' Anno domini 1626.

Roger Veritie & Agnes foster were marryed June the xj$^{th}$
Robert Brogstonn & Elizabeth West were marryed Januarie the xxij$^{th}$

Nomina pueroru' baptizandoru' anno p$^{r}$dicto.

Anne the daughter of Thomas Hebden was bap : June the xxv$^{th}$
Christofer the sonne of John Settle of Conishtonn was bap : July the xiij$^{th}$
John the sonne of George Horner was bap : Januarie the xij$^{th}$
Jeane the daughter of Christofer Jacksonn was bap : Februarie the xxv$^{th}$
John the sonno of Roger Stonay was bap : March the xvj$^{th}$

Nomina defunctoru' eode' anno.

Two Infants the Children of Christopher Wade were buryed Aprill y$^{e}$ 3$^{d}$

Nomina sponsaliu' Anno domini 1627.

Richard Battie & Issabell Thompsonn were marryed Apryll the xxviij$^{th}$
Thomas Marshall & Alice West were marryed May the xxviij$^{th}$
John Jacksonn & Elizabeth Canny were marryed June the vij$^{th}$

nomina pueroru' baptiz Anno p$^{r}$dicto.

Willyã the sonne of Christofer Wade was bap : Apryll the xxij$^{th}$
Jeane the daughter of Anthonie Ward was bap : June the xviij$^{th}$
Margret the daughter of Thomas Marshall was bap : August the xviij$^{th}$
Christofer Costentyne the sonne of Lawrence was bap : September y$^{e}$ xvj$^{th}$
Susanna the daughter of Henry Ibbotsonn was bap : October y$^{e}$ xxx$^{th}$
Henry the sonn of John Laylande was bap : March the vj$^{th}$
Richard the sonne of Richard Battie was bap : March the v$^{th}$

nomina defunctoru'.

Willyã the sonne of Christopher Wade was buryed June the iiij$^{th}$
Jeane the daughter of Christofer Jacksonn was buryed Nouember the xxv$^{th}$
Margret the daughter of Thomas Marshall was buryed December the second.
An Infant the daughter of Thomas Hebden was buryed Januarie the xvj$^{th}$
Willyã Ripplay of Conistonn was buryed Januarie the xx$^{th}$
Elizabeth the wyfe of Thomas Hebden was buryed January the xxj$^{th}$
Anne the daughter of Edward Warde was buryed Februarie the seconde.

Nomina sponsaliu' Anno domini 1628.

John Battie & Issabell Wiggleswoorth were marryed Julie the xxij$^{th}$

Nomina pueroru' bap : Anno p$^{r}$dicto.

Agnes the daughter of Thomas Layland was bap : Apryll the vj$^{th}$
Marie the daughter of Christofer Jacksonn was bap : September the 7$^{th}$
Agnes the daughter of Robert Costentyne was bap : Nouember the 17$^{th}$
Margret the daughter of Roger Franckland was bap : Januarie the 18$^{th}$
Christofer the sonne of Thomas Marshall March the fyrst.

Nomina defunctoru' anno p$^{r}$dicto.

John Kydd als Howsonn was buryed Januarie the xx$^{th}$
John Tennant Clark preacher of the woord was buryed Januarie the xxj$^{th}$

nomina sponsaliu' Anno domini 1629.

Thomas Ellisse & marie Layland were marryed August the third.

nomina pueroru' baptiz : eodē' anno.

Thomas the sonne of John Lambart was bap : Apryll the xxvij$^{th}$
Margret the base borne daughter of Gennet Ibbotsonn August the xxx$^{th}$
Robert the sonne of John Battie was bap : October the xxv$^{th}$

nomina defunctoru' eode' anno viz 1629. [A fol. 7. v.

Jeane Hoddgsonn was buryed Apryll the xiiij$^{th}$
Jeane the daughter of Anthonie Ward was buryed May the 26$^{th}$
Mathew Hewit was buryed in the Chappell August the vj$^{th}$
Thomas the sonne of John Lambart was buryed October the xiiij$^{th}$
Issabell the daughter of Lawrence Layland Februarie the last.

nomina sponsaliu' Anno domini 1630.

Robert Layland & Elizabeth Horner were marryed Nouember the viij^th^
Mathew Hewit & Margret Inman were marryed Januarie y^e^ syxt.

Nomina pueroru' baptiz: anno p^r^dicto.

Dorethie the daughter of Anthonie Ward was bap: Apryll the xv^th^
Thomas the sonne of Richard Ayretonn was bap: May the xvj^th^
Thomas the sonne of George Horner was bap: September y^e^ 26^th^
Lawrence the sonne of Lawrence Costentyne was bap: December the xix^th^

Nomina defunctoru' anno p^r^dicto.

Gennet the wyfe of Thomas Settle was buryed June the viij^th^
An Infante the childe of a stranger June the xviij^th^
John the sonne of Richard Lambarte was buryed June the xx^th^
Margerie Wilkinsonn the widdow of Symon Wilkinsonn buryed October y^e^ viij^th^
Elizabeth the wyfe of Richard Layland was buryed Nouember the xiij^th^
Margret the daughter of Robert Costentyne was buryed Nouember y^e^ xvj^th^
Robert Slinger was buryed the xxvij^th^ day of December.
Issabell the wyfe of John Battie was buryed the iiij^th^ day of Februarie.
John the sonne of George Horner was buryed March the seconde.

Nomina pueroru' baptizandoru' Anno domini 1631.

John the sonne of Roger Franckland was bap: Januarie y^e^ first.
Margret the daughter of Robert Layland was bap: Januarie the x^th^
Thomas the sonne of John Layland was bap: March the xxvj^th^
Henry the sonn of Mathew Hewit was bap: Apryll the third.
Francis the sonne of Thomas Layland was bap: Julie the x^th^
Agnes the daughter of xpopher Jacksonn was bap: Julie the x^th^
Margret the daughter of Robert Layland was bap: Januari the x^th^
John the sonne of Roger Franckland was bap: Januarie the first.

nomina defunctoru' anno p^r^dicto.

Anne the wyfe of John Willsonn was buried August the xx^th^
John Willsonn of Conishtonn was buryed Nouember the third.
John (?) the sonne of Roger Franckland was buryed March the xvj^th^
Dorethie Witham was buryed March the xvj^th^

Nomina pueroru' bap: Anno domini 1632.

Elizabeth the daughter of Roger Stonay March the 25^th^
Edward Warde the sonne of Anthonie Ward Nouember the 25^th^
George the sonne of Roger Franckland March the x^th^

Nomina defunctoru' anno p^r^dicto.

Thomas Battie was buryed July the viij^th^ 1632.

Nomina sponsaliu' Anno domini 1633.

John Atkinsonn & Elizabeth Lynsay were marryed June the x^th^
Robert Battie & Margret Atchinsonn were marryed July the xiiij^th^
Robert Demesce & Hellen Gray were marryed September y^e^ x^th^

nomina pueroru' baptiz : anno p^r^dicto.

Margret the daughter of John Lambart was bap : March y^e^ last.
Willyã the sonne of Mathew Hewit was bap : August the xj^t^
Agnes the daughter of Richard Ayretonn was bap : December the viij^th^
Margret the daughter of Henry Costentyne Februarie the xiij^th^
[John the sonne of Thomas Hebden Januarie the 26^th^]

Nomina defunctoru' anno p^r^dicto.

Willyã Slinger was buryed Apryll the xij^th^
Willyã Markendayle was buryed May the xxx^th^
Richard Layland was buryed the laste day of Auguste.
The base borne childe of Jeane Hodgsonn buryed Septem : y^e^ v^th^
Thomas Franckland was buryed December the xx^th^
Peter Pullayne was buryed Jannarie the xix^th^

Nomina sponsaliu' Anno domini 1634.

Steauen Maudslay & Agnes Tennant were married June the xviij^th^
Thomas Clarke & Margret Jacksonn were marryed June the laste.
Abrahã Snell & Margret Ibbotsonn were marryed Septb^r^ y^e^ 3^th^
Robert Seward & Gennet Settle were married Januari the 27^th^

Nomina pueroru' bap : Anno p^r^dicto.

Francis the sonne of John Battie was bap : March the xxix^th^
James the sonne of John Layland was bap : May the xj^th^
Frances the daughter of George Horner May the fyrst.

nomina pueroru' bap : Anno p^r^dicto viz. 1634. [A fol. 8. r.

Elizabeth the daughter of Christofer Jacksonn bap : September y^e^ 14^th^
Margret the daughter of Robert Demeasen bap : Julie the vj^th^
Issabell the daughter of Robert Layland bap : October the xiij^th^
Gennet the daughter of Roger Stonay bap : December the xiiij^th^
Diana the daughter of Thomas Layland bap : December the xxj^th^

Nomina defunctoru' eode' Anno.

Agnes the daughter of Robert Costentyne was buryed May the thirde.
Agnes the wyfe of Robert Costentyne was buryed September the xxvij^th^
Margret the wyfe of George Tennant buryed October the ix^th^
Alice the wyfe of John Layland buryed December the x^th^
Anne the wyfe of George Horner buryed December the xxix^th^
John Layland was buryed Januarie the viij^th^
Margret the wyfe of Robert Slinger buryed Januarie the xxvij^th^
John Snell was buryed Februarie the xxj^th^
Francis Wade was buryed March the xxj^th^

Nomina sponsaliu' Anno domini 1635.

George Horner & Margret Franckland marryed August the xvij^th^
John Waylock & Alice Lambart marryed September the xxj^th^
Edward Hartlay & Margret Layland marryed Nouember the xxx^th^

nomina pueroru' bap : anno p^r^dicto.

Alice the daughter of Roert Wigglesworth bap : October the iiij^th^
Christofer the sonne of John Lambart October the xviij^th^

Issabell the daughter of Henry Costentyne October the xxv$^{th}$
Thomas the sonne of Anthonie Ward bap: Nouember the xxxj$^{th}$
Grace the daughter of John Battie bap: Januarie the xxj$^{th}$

Nomina defunctoru' anno p$^{r}$dicto.

Issabell Ayretonn was buryed March the 29$^{th}$
Alice the daughter of Robert Wigglesworth buryed October xxvj$^{th}$
Issabell the daughter of Henry Costentyne buryed Januarie the seconde.
Margret Todde widdow was buryed Januarie the fourth.
Elizabeth Todd was buryed Januarie the fyfte.
Susanna the wyfe of Richard Todd buryed Januarie the xix$^{th}$
Thomas Franckland was buryed Januarie the xxj$^{th}$
Margret the daughter of Richard Todd was buryed Februarie the xxiij$^{th}$
Christopher the sonne of Henry Thompsonn was buryed March the vj$^{th}$

Nomina sponsaliu' Anno domini 1636.

George Bramo and Margret Windsor were marryed September the 21$^{th}$
John Sydgsweek and Elizabeth Linsay were marryed Nouember the 28$^{th}$

Nomina pueroru' baptiz: Anno domini 1636.

Alice the daughter of Matthew Hewitt was bap: Aprill the x$^{th}$
Robert the sonne of Willyā Slinger was bap: June the 5$^{th}$
Margrett the daughter of George Horner was bap: Julie the x$^{th}$
Phillip the sonne of Thomas Londsdayle was bap: September the xxv$^{th}$
Ann the daughter of Robert Wiggleswoorth was bap: October the xx$^{th}$
James the sonne of Willyā Tennant was bap: Nouember the vj$^{th}$
Margrett the daughter of George Bramo was bap: December y$^{e}$ first.
Frances the daughter of Roger Franckland was bap: December y$^{e}$ iiij$^{th}$
Elizabeth the daughter of Henry Costentyne was bap: December y$^{e}$ xiiij$^{th}$
Alice the daughter of Thomas Hebden was bap: March the xxij$^{th}$

Nomina defunctoru' Anno domini 1636.

Mabell Wiggleswoorth widdow was buryed March the xxx$^{th}$
Margrett Tennante was buryed Aprill the xxvj$^{th}$
Richard Lambart was buryed Julie the xvij$^{th}$
Richard Costentyne yonger was buried Julie the xxvj$^{th}$
George Tennant was buryed Auguste the viij$^{th}$
Phillipp Londsdayle was buryed December the vij$^{th}$
Hellen Thompsonn widdow was buryed December the ix$^{th}$
Agnes Costentyne widdow was buryed December the xxx$^{th}$
Ann Infant the sonne of Robert Layland was buryed Feb 28$^{th}$

Nomina pueroru' baptiz: Anno domini 1637.

Anthonie the sonne of Roger Stonay was baptized Aprill the xvj$^{th}$
Cutbert the sonne of Christofer Thompsonn was bap: Aprill the xxiij$^{th}$
Georg the sonne of John Tennante was bap: May the xiiij$^{th}$
John the sonne of Thomas Lynsay was bap: August the xiij$^{th}$
Lawrence the sonne of Edward Hartlay was bap: August the xvj$^{th}$
Elizabeth the daughter of Thomas Londsdayle was bap: Nouember the xij$^{th}$

Margret the daughter of Christopher Jacksonn was bap: December y^e^ x^th^
Hellen the daughter of Robert Layland was bap: March the iiij^th^

Nomina pueroru' baptiz: anno p'dicto viz. 1637. [A fol. 8. v.

Jeane the daughter of Richard Ayretoun was bap: March the vij^th^
Willyã the sonne of Willyã West was baptiz: March the xiiij^th^

Nomina Sponsaliu' Anno p'dicto viz. 1637.

Robert Battie & Alice Wigglesworth were Marryed Julie the xxv^th^
Thomas Riplay & Elizabeth Sydgswecke were Married Nouember the vij^th^
Robert Middlebrough & Gennet Ibbotsonn were marryed Januarie y^e^ xiiij^th^
John Laylande & margret Costentyne were Marryed Januarie the xxix^th^

Nomina defunctoru' Anno p'dicto viz: 1637.

Alice the wyfe of Richard Layland was buryed March the last day.
Richard Costentyne thelder was buryed Apryll the fyrst day.
Thomas Hartlay was buryed Apryll the vij^th^
Anthonie the sonne of Roger Stonay was buryed may the iiij^th^
Margret the daughter of John Lambarte was buryed Julie the xxv^th^
Thomas Settle was buryed Julie the xxviij^th^
John Horner was buryed December the xviij^th^
Hellen Settle widdow was buryed Januarie the thirde.
Robert Costentyne was buryed Januarie the x^th^
Thomas Layland was buryed Januarie the xxvj^th^

Nomina pueroru' baptizandoru' Anno domini 1638.

Margret the daughter of Robert Battie was baptised May the 27^th^
James the sonne of Anthonie Warde was baptised May the 29^th^
Richard the sonne of Robert middlebrough was bap: June the 20^th^
Issabell the daughter of Roger Stonay was bap: Julie the 8^th^
Issabell the daughter of John Lambarte was bap: Julie the 11^th^
Gennett the daughter of George Horner was bap: October the 28^th^
Elizabeth the daughter of George Brãmo was bap: Januari 27^th^
Thomas the sonne of Matthew Hewitt was bap: Februarie the 10^th^
Ann the daughter of James Rayner was bap: Februarie y^e^ 24^th^
Willyã the sonne of Willyã Slinger was bap: March y^e^ 10^th^

Nomina defunctoru' Anno 1638.

James the sonne of Anthonie Ward was buryed June y^e^ 20^th^
John Settle was buryed December the thirde.
Hellen the daughter of Robert Layland was buryed Januarie y^e^ 5^th^
An Infante of Robert Wiggleswoorthes vnbaptised borne & buryed Febru: 11^th^
Margret the wyfe of Robert Wiggleswoorth was buryed Feb: 15^th^

Nomina pueroru' baptizandoru' Anno domini 1639.

Anne the daughter of Cuthbert Wade was baptized August the xj^th^
Jeane the daughter of Roger Franckland bap: Nouember the third.
Marie the daughter of Robert Laylande was bap: Nouember the thirde.

Margret the daughter of John Tennante was bap: Nouember the tenth.
Jennet the daughter of John Layland was bap: Nouember the 17th
Richard the sonne of Henry Costentyne was bap: Januarie the xijth
Christofer the sonne of Richard Thompsonn was bap: Januarie the xixth
Thomas the sonne of Christofer Thompsonn was bap: March the iiijth

Nomina defunctoru' Anno p'dicto.

Willyā the sonne of John Laylande was buryed March the 25th
Richard Layland was buryed Aprill the 5th
Margret the wyfe of Edward Hartlay was buryed Apryll the 25th
Hellen the wyfe of Thomas Lynsay was buryed Julie the ixth
Jennet the wyfe of Robert Middlebrooke was buryed December the vijth
Jeane the wyfe of Christofer Ibbotsonn was buryed Januarie the vijth

Nomina Sponsaliu' Anno domini 1610.

Christofer Caluard & Elizabeth Etheringtonn were marryed June the 15th
Robert Wigglesworth & Alice Procter were marryed August the third.
Roger Wilde & Anne Mosse were marryed August the syxt.

Nomina pueroru' baptizandoru' Anno domini 1610.

John the sonne of Willya Tennant was baptized May the third.
Elizabeth the daughter of Cuthbert Wade was baptized September the third.
[John the sonne of Thomas Ripplay was bap: September the 14th]
Richard the sonne of Willyā Tennant was bap: December the 25th
[Christofer the sonne of Robert Sydgsweck was bap: Nouember the 5th]
John the sonne of John Lambert was bap: December the 28th
Joseph the sonne of Thomas Londsdayle was bap: Januarie the fyrst.
Agnes the daughter of Robert Costentyne was bap: Januarie the 10th
Agnes the daughter of George Horner was baptiz: Januarie the last.

Nomina defunctoru' in Anno domini 1610. [A fol. 9. r.

Margret Snell widdow was buryed Apryll the 8th
Anne Lambert late wyfe of Richard Lambert was buryed Apryll the 15th
Thomas the sonne of Matthew Huit was buryed Aprill the 16th
Hellen the wyfe of Lawrence Layland was buryed June the 17th
An Infante vnbaptized of Henry Procters was buryed August the thirde.
Willyā Butcher a souldier of Captayne Paries band buried Feb: the third.
Two Infants vnbaptiz: the sonne and daughter of John Sidgsweck buried Feb: 13th
Margrett the late wyfe of Richard Pullayne was buryed Februarie the 25th

Nomina pueroru' baptizandoru' in Anno domini 1611.

Jone the daughter of George Brāmo was baptized Aprill the 4th
John the sonne of Matthew Hewit was bap: Aprill the xjth
Robert the sonne of Anthonie Ward was bap: Aprill the 15th
Margret the daughter of Robert Wigglesworth baptiz August 17th
Robert the sonne of Richard Costentyne bap: September the 29th

Elizabeth the daughter of Willyã Slinger bap : October the 9th
Issabel the daughter of John Layland bap : Januarie the 3d

Nomina Defunctoru' in anno domini 1641.

Jeane the daughter of Roger Franckland buried March 25th
John Tennant was buryed May the 20th
Issabell Costentyne was buried June the first.
Elizabeth Ibbotsonn was buryed June the 24th
Agnes the wyfe of Roger Stonay was buryed June the 27th
Margret the daughter of Willyã Tennant Julie the 4th
Willyã Slinger was buried Julie the 14th
Christofer the sonne of Richard Thompsonn buried August the 18th
Margret the daughter of Robert Wiggleswoorth buried August 30th
Edward Ward was buried in the Church October 14th payd iijs 4d to Edward Hartlay & Thomas Hebden by Thomas Ward his sonne.
Issabell the wyfe of Thomas Kydd buried Nouember 15th

Nomina puerorū' baptizandorū' Anno domini 1642.

Thomas the sonne of Robert Wiggleswoorth bap : August the first.
Christofer the sonne of Cutbert Wade was baptized September the 21th
John the sonn of George Horner bap : Februarie the 19th
Margret the daughter of Robert Costentyne bap : March the 12th

Nomina defunctorū' Anno 1642.

Margret the base begotten daughter of Gennet Ibbotsonn was buried September ye 17th

nomina puerorū' bap : Anno 1643.

Elizabeth the daughter of Willyã Tennant was baptized Januarie the 28th
[Henry the sonne of Richard Costentyne was bap : Aprill the 7th]
Dorethie the daughter of Richard Franckland was baptized June the 25th
Elias Windsor the sonne of Elias Windsor was bap : Julie the 15th
Isabell the daughter of Henry Costentyne was baptized June the 25th
Alice ye daughter of Go : Layland jun. was baptized December (?) 20th

Nomina defunctorū' 1643.

Henry Costentyne the sonne of Richard Costentyne was buried October the 20th
Jone the daughter of George Bramo buried Januarie the 20th

Nomina puerorū' bap : Anno 1644.

Magdalen the daughter of Henry Garforth was bap : Januarie 19th
Agnes the daughter of Richard Thompsonn was bap : Februarie the 20th
Elizabeth the daughter of Willya Tennant March the 7th

Nomina defunctorū' 1644.

Elizabeth Londsdayle was buryed Nouember the 28th
Margret the wyfe of George Horner was buried Januarie the 19th
Christofer Drake was buried October the 27th

Nomina sponsaliu 1645.

Richard Battie & Jeane Hodgsonn were marryed may the first.

Nomina pueroru' bap: 1645.

Agnes the daughter of Richard Costentyne was baptized October the 15th
Willyã the sonne of John Layland was bap: October the 27th
Margret the daughter of John Sidgsweek bap: Nouember the 23th
John the sonn of Elias Windsor was bap: March 15th
Francis the daughter of John Layland was bap: March the 17th

Nomina defunctoru' Anno 1645. [A fol. 9. v.

Margret the late wyfe of Edward Warde was buried Aprill the 16th
James Tennant was buried Aprill the 17th
Issabell the wyfe of Thomas Costentyne was buried October the 22th
Elizabeth the wyfe of John Sidgsweeke was buried Nouember the 23th
Margret the daughter of John Sidgsweek was buried December the 14th
Jeane the wyfe of Richard Battie was buried Januarie the 28.

Nomina sponsaliu' Anno 1646.

Willyã Gill & Anne Whiteker were marryed June the 14th
Richard Battie & Anne Windsor wer married September the 10th

Nomina pueroru' baptizandoru' Anno 1646.

Margret the daughter of Richard Todd bap: May the 3th
Richard the sonne of Edward Broadbelt bap: May the 10th
John the sonne of Willyã Tennant of Conistonn bap: June the 19th
Samuell the sonne of Willyã Tennant bap: August the seconde.
John the sonne of Henry Costentyne bap: August the 9th
Margret the daughter of Richard Franckland bap: Nouember the 22th
Agnes the daughter of Mr Cutbert Wade bap: December the 21th
Hellen the daughter of Robert Wiggleswoorth bap: December ye 23th
Grace the daughter of John Sidgsweek bap: December the 28th
Alice the daughter of George Bramo bap: March the 12th

Nomina Defunctoru' Anno 1646.

Agnes the daughter of Mr Cutbert Wade was buryed June the 10th
Richard the sonne of Edward Broadbelt was buried June the 14th
Willyã the sonne of John Laylande senior was buried Januarie ye 16th

Nomina pueroru' baptiz Anno domini 1647.

Elizabeth the daughter of Edwarde Broadebelt was bap: Aprill 28.
John the sonne of Robert Sygsweek was baptized May the 23th
Issabell the daughter of Robert Costentyne bap: June the 24th
John the sonn of Willyã Paylay baptized Februarie the 20th

Nomina defunctoru' Anno 1647.

Thomas Settle was buried Aprill the 29th
John Linsay was buried June the 15th
Elizabeth the daughter of Edward Broadbelt was buried Julie the 22th
Thomas Linsay was buried Januarie the 4th
John Collisonn was buried Januarie the 28th
Elizabeth Stonay widdow was buried Februarie 13th
Anne Rayner widdow was buried.

Nomina pueroru' baptizandoru' Anno 1648.

Marie the daughter of M^r Cuthbart Wade May the xviij^th
James the sonn of John Sydgsweek Julie the xxvj^th
Thomas Veritie the sonne of Cuthbert Veritie August the vj^th
Margret the daughter of Richard Costentyne September the iij^th
[Dorethie the daughter of Edward Broadbelt October 26^th]
Susanna the daughter of Richard Tod Nouember the xxvj^th
Hellen the daughter of Henry Costentyne Januari x^th
Richard the sonn of Willyā Tennant Januarie the xxij^th

nomina defunctoru' Anno 1648.

Anne Rayner widdow was buryed Aprill the xiij^th
Elizabeth Layland Aprill the last.
Willyā Lynsay buried May the third.
Margret y^e wyfe of M^r Christopher Wade Januarie the 22^th
Elizabeth the wyfe of M^r Anthonie Ward Januarie the 29.

Nomina pueroru' baptizandoru' Anno domini 1649.

Cuthbart the sonn of Willyā Holiday & Elizabeth Costentine bap: March the 26^th
Elizabeth the daughter of Robert Wiggleswoorth bap: Aprill 15^th
Hanna the daughter of Willyā Tennant bap: Aprill 22^th
Hellen the daughter of Henry Costentine bap:
Mary the daughter of George Bramo May the 7^th
Edwarde (?) the sonn of Willyā Tennant bap:
Thomas the sonne of Thomas Costentyne bap: Februari the 7^th

Nomina defunctoru' eode' Anno.

Elizabeth the daughter of Robert Wiggleswoorth sepulta October 29^th
Elias Windsor sepultus September the 5^th

Nomina pueroru' baptizandoru' Anno domini 1650.

Sara the daughter of M^r Cuthbart Wayde baptized May the 5^th
Grace the daughter of John Sidgsweeke baptized August the first.
John the sonne of John Layland senior bap: October the 6^th

Anno p^rdicto 1650. [A fol. 10. r.

Issabell the daughter of Richard Franckland bap: October the 13^th
Richard Wigglesworth y^e sonne of Robert Wigglesworth bap: Nouember the 10^th
Hellen the daughter of Francis Layland bap: Nouember the 26^th
Marie the daughter of Edward Broadbelt bap: March the 28^th

Nomina defunctoru' Anno 1650.

Anne the wyfe of Richard Todd sepulta Aprill the 4^th
John Graunge sepultus nouember the 10^th
Mathew Hewit sepultus Januarie the 15^th
Edward the sonne of Anthonie Warde sepult Februarie the 16^th in temp.
Robert the sonne of Richard Costentyne sepult: March the 5^th
George Horner sepultus March the 10^th
John the sonne of Willyā Tennant of Coniston sepult March 13^th
Thomas the sonne of George Horner sepult March the 19^th

Nomina pueroru' baptizandoru' 1651.

Thomas the sonne of Richard Costentyne baptized Aprill the 18th
Jenet the daughter of Henry Costentyne baptiz Nouember the 30th

Nomina defunctoru' Anno p'dicto viz : 1651.

Thomasin the wyfe of Richard Costentine buried Aprill the 20th
Frances Costentine was buried Julie 27th
Margret Tennat the wyfe of James Tennant was buried June the 7th
Richard Broadbelt was buryed Julie 27th
Sara Wade was buried Julie the 14th
The wyfe of Anthonie Bouch was buried October 15th
Alice Hewit was buried Nouember the 14th
Dina Layland was buried Nouember the 24th
Anthonie Ibbotsonn was buried Nouember the 30th
Willyã Ayretonn was buried Januarie the xjth
Issabell the wyfe of Richard Battie was buried Januarie 28th
An Infant of Willyam Tennants was buried March the 24th
Richard Johnsonn was buried March the 14th

Nomina pueroru' baptizandoru' Anno 1652.

John the sonn of Richard Thompsonn baptized Aprill the 12th
Charles the sonn of George Bramo baptized June the 6th
Agnes the daughter of Francis Layland baptized Januarie the vjth
Thomas the sonn of Christofer Settle bap : December the 9th
Jeane the daughter of Thomas Costentine bap : Januari the 23th
John the sonn of Willyã Tennant bap : Februarie the 13th
Margret the daughter of Robert Wiggleswoorth bap : Feb : the vjth

Nomina defunctoru' Anno 1652.

Issabell Costentine widdow was buried Aprill the vjth
Marie the daughter of Edwarde Broadbelt buried Julie the 27th
John the sonn of John Layland was buried October the first.
Marie the daughter of John Sidgsweek buried October the 9th
Willyam Prestonn Nouember the 27th
Elizabeth Hodgsonn December the 12th
Issabell Thompsonn the wyfe of Christofer Thompsonn Januarie the 12th
Robart Layland buried Januarie the 24th
John Lambart Januarie the 26th

Nomina sponsaliu' Anno domini 1652.

John Shackleton & Jeane Hall married Januari the 12th 1652.

Nomina pueroru' baptizandoru'.

Christofer the sonne of Edward Broadbelt bap : June the sixteenth.
Hellen the daughter of John Layland senior.
Cutbart the sonne of Cutbard Wade bap : September the 20th
Francis the sonne of Richard Battie bap : Januarie the 25.
[Robert the sonne of John Ibbotsone bap : August ye 14th 1655].
* Edward ye sonne of Laurence Hartley bap : Aug : ye 14th 1655.

* This entry is written along the margin of the page.

Nomina defunctoru' eodem anno.

George Ward was buryed June the 10th
Robart Franckland was buried.
Mrs Agnes the wyfe of Mr Cutbart Wad was buried September the 17th
Susanna the daughter of Richard Todd.
Anthonie Ward was buried Nouember the 20th

nomina pueror' baptizandorm Año : Dom : 1656.

Katharina filia Thomæ Warde baptiz : fuit tricesima die Aprillis 1656.
Will filius Matthew Hewit defunct .........

Anno domini 1657. [A fol. 10. v.

Henry the sonne of Thomas Ibbotsonn was buried Aug : The fifth.
Henry the sonne of Thomas Ibbotsonn Minister of the worde of god at the Chappell of Conishton fiftie three yeares and vpwards and was buried the Nynth day of Januarie.

Nomina pueroru' Baptizandoru' An : Do : 1657.

Lawrence son of William Holiday November 22th

Nomina defunctoru' Anno 1657.

An Infant ye son of Henery Hewit of Conistone March 11th
Christopher Thomson of Outgang March 19th

Nomina Baptizandoru' Anno 1657.

Thomas son of Francis Layland Frebruary 22th
Isabell Daughter of Richard Battie March ...th

Nomina pueroru' Baptizandoru' 1658.

John Son of Richard Costentine May 23th
John Son of Edward Broadbelt June 6th
Anthony Son of Thomas Warde of Northcoat June 24th
Henery Son of Thomas Ibbotson August 22th
Anne Daughter of Thomas Costentine of Kilnsay Octo : 6.
Anne Daughter of Robert Wiglesworth Nouem : 7th
Richard son of Robert Costentine December 12th

Nomina Defunctoru' 1658.

Jenet Wife of Willm Layland Aug : 10th
Edward Broadbelt of Kilnsay Nov : 25th
Jenet ye Daughter of Rodger Stoney Feb : 4th

Nomina Baptizandoru' 1659.

Margret ye Daughter of Laurence Hartlay Apr : 4th
Margret ye Daughter of Christopher Settle May 22th
Margret ye Daughter of Henery Hewit Nov : 20th
John ye Son of Willm Schatshar Janru : 20th
Richard Son of Richard Costentine Feb : 5th
Elizabeth ye Daughter of Michaell Airton Mar : 11th
Rodger Son of Thomas Warde March 13th

Nomina Sponsaliu' 1659.

Will' Tophan of Grissington and Isabell Lambert of Kilnsay were married Octo : 6th

Nomina Defunctoru' 1659.

Alice Wife of Henery Ibbotson Decem : ij[th]
Jane Britton of Kilnsay Jaña : 8[th]
Elizabeth Daughter of Henery Costentine Jaña : 19.

Nomina puerorum 1668. [A fol. 11. r.

Thomas the sonne Christopher Lambert bap : 26[th] of Aprill.
Elline the Daughter of John Heseldon bap : 17[th] of May.
John the sonne of Richard Battie bap : 23[th] of August.
Abigall the Daughter of Richard Peart bap : 6[th] of Sep :
Gennet the daughter of Christopher Sidgeweeke bap : in Jan.
Matthew the sonne of Lenord huit baptized the 10[th] of Januarie.
John the sonne of James Tennant bap : 10[th] of Aprill :

Nomina Defunctoru'.

Roger the sonne of Roger Stonay buried 20[th] of October.

Nomina Puer' Anno Dominic 1669.

Elizabeth the daughter of Robert Slinger baptiz : the 30[th] of May.
Elizabeth the daughter of John Heseldon baptiz : the 25[th] of december.

Nomina Sponsalium.

Henric Rimmi'tone and Elizabeth Mayson was maried the 2 : Auguste.

Nomina Defunctorum.

Alis the wife of Robert Slinger buried the 9[th] day of September.
Elizabeth the wife of Willyã Shaw buried the 16 day of Nouember.
Alis the wife of Robert Wiggleworth buried the 4[th] day of Januarie.
Elizabeth the daughter of Robert Slinger buried 20[th] of Februarie.

Nomina puerorn' Anno Dominic 1670.

Jonathan the sonne of John Hewit baptiz : the 12[th] day of June.
Elline the daughter of Christopher Lambarte bap : 18[th] day of septemb[r]
Richard the sonne of John Horner baptiz : the 24[th] day of July.
Thomas the sonne of Henric Rimmi'tone bap : the 26[th] day of March.
Alis the Daughter of Christopher Sidgeweeke bap : March the xxvj[th]

Nomina Sponsaliu'.

Willyam Weste and Agnes Branmo Maried the 11[th] of Julij.

Nomina Defunctoru'.

John the sonne of Willyam Tennante buried the 4[th] day of May.
Alis the wife of Thomas Ibbotsonne buried the 21[th] day of June.
Richard Tompson the sonne of Henry Tomp : buried 20[th] day of August.
Margret the wife of Robert Pullane buried the 22[th] day of Auguste.

Nomina sponsaliu' Anno dominic 1671.

Thomas Ibbotsonn and Doritie Shipperd was Maried May the ij[th]

Nomina pueroru'.

Agnes the daughter of John Heseldon bap : August 20[th]

Nomina defunctoru'

Alis the wife of Henry Costentyne buried August 20th
George the sonne of John Tennante buried Aprill 7th

Nomic. puerorn' Anno Domine 1672.

Tho: the sonne of mr Tho: Warde bap: the 9th day of June.
Anthonie Ibbotson sonne of Tho: Ibbot: bap 12th october.
Elisabeth the daughter of Chr: Lam: bapd Jan (?): 13th

Nomine Sponsaliu' eodem Anno. [A fol. 11. v.

John Cookeson and Elline Layland Maried 20th of April.
Robert Slinger and Alis Hebden Maried 11th of May.
Christopher Cost: and Anne Stonay Maried June 8th

Nomine defunctoru' 1672.

Alis daughter of Christ: Sidg: buried the 2th of May.
Elisabeth Sidg: the wife of Christopher buried 21th May.
Henry Rimm'ton buried the 28th day of October.
Francis the sonne of Samuell Wade buried 24th Decem:
Edward Hartlay the sonne of Lawrence buried 3th of Janu:
Mr Roger Warde of Northcote buried 25th of Februa.
Mr Christopher the sonne of Arthur Wade buried 9th of March.
Elisabeth the daughter of Chr: Lambert buried 13th of March.

[Anno Dommini 1673.]

Frances the daughter of John Horner buried 17th of Aprill.
Frances the daugher of Robert Slinger buried 8th of Apri.
*Anthonie the sonne of Tho: Ibbot: buried the first of May.
Richard the Sonne of John Horner buried 21th of Aprill.
Memerandum that Mr Tho: Warde payde iijs 4d for his Fathers buriall in the Chappell of Conishton to Micaell Setle and Christopher Costentine Churchwardens for the yere aboue writen.

Anno Dominic 1673 Nomine puerorum.

Edwarde the sonne of John Heseldon bap: Nouember the 9th
John the sonne of Christopher Mallesone bap: Januarie the vth
Mary the Daugh'er of John Huit bap: Aprill the 5th

Nominie sponsalium.

Christopher Awecoke and Elisabeth Coulton Maried Nouem: xiijth

Nominie defunctoru'.

Anthonie the sonne of Thomas Ibbotson buried may the first.
Jeane the wife of Lawrence Costentyne buried Nouem: xxxth
Francis the sonne of John battie buried the xxiijth of Januarie.
Alis the daughter of Robert Costentine buried xxiiijth Jan:

Anno Domm' 1674.

Susanna the daughter of Tho: Ibbot: bap: may the first.
John the sonne of John Winder bap: September the xth
Elisabeth the daughter of Thomas Car bap: Octo: 11th
margret the Daughter of Christopher Lambart bap: Febr: 28th

* Ruled out.

Nomia defunctoru'.

Anne the daughter of Richard battie buried May 21th
Lawrence the sonne of Thomas Setle buried decem 2th

Nomina Puero' 1675. [A fol. 12. r.

Agnes the daughter of John Wincer bap: September the 5th
Margret the daughter of Christopher Malison bap: Jannarie the 16.

Nomina Defunctoru'.

Robert the sonne of Richard Pullane buried September the first.
Henrie Huit buried Nouember the fourteenth.
Margret Huit widdow was buried Nouember the 18th
Lawrence the sonne of Thomas Costentyne buried December 20th

Nomina Pueroru' bap: Anno Dom: 1676.

John the sonn of John Hesletine bap: May 10th day.

Nomina Defunctoru' eodem Anno.

Robert the sonn of Willi' Sidgwicke buried January 6th day.
Willi' ye sonn of James Teñant buried August 11th day.

Nomina sponsaliu' Anno Dom: 1677.

Christopher Iveson & Ellin Constentine married January 17th day.
Cuthbert sonn of Willi' Holyday & Margret Ibbotson mar: Janu: 22th day.

1356225

Nomina Pueroru' bap: eodem Anno.

Agnes ye daughter of John Winder: bap: Septem: 9th day.
Thomas the sonn of Thomas Ibbotsonn bap: 6th of October.
Isabell the daughter of Christopher Lambert bap: Octob: 7th day.
Alice the daughter of John Winser bap: 28th of October.
Margret the daughter of John Hebden bap: Decem: 23d day.
Robert the sonn of Christopher Mallesonn bap: Janu: 6th day.
Ann ye daughter of Richard Batty bap: 13th of January.
Thomas the sonn of Leonard Gildard bap: Feb: 7th day.
Margret the daughter of Thomas Watson bap: March 10th day.

Nomina Defunctoru' eodem Anno.

Alise daughter of John Hebden buried January 26th day.
Margret the wife of Thomas Holmes buried Feb: 7th day.
Alise the daughter of John Winser buried Feb: 27th day.

Nomina Sponsalium Anno Domi: 1678 &

Nomina Pueroru' bap: eodem Anno 1678.

Alice ye daughter of Rich: Wiglesworth bap: June 9th day.
Christopher ye sonn of Cuthbert Holiday bap: Novem: 18th day.

Nomina defunctorum eodem Anno: 78.

Agnes Winser buried May 20th day 1678.
Willi' Tennant buried Janu: 5th day: & an Affidavit delivered Janu: 10th day Anno Dom: 1678.
Margret Tompson buried Janu: 15th day and an Affidavit delivered Janu: 23 1678.

The Infant child John Hesledins buried Feb : 24th & an Affidavit delivered Feb : 28 1678.
The Infant child of Agnes Verity buried March 6th & an Affidavit delivered March 12th 1678.

Nomina Pueroru' : bap : 1679. [A fol. 12. v.

Henry ye sonn of Henry Robinson bap : Aprill 27 : 1679.
James the sonn of Christo : Malesonn : bap : Augus : 7th 1679.
Margret the daughter of John Winser : bap : Sep : 7 : 79.
Anthony son of Tho : Ibbotsonn : bap : Decem : 21 : 79.
Tho the son of John Hesletine bap : March 8th : 79.

Nomina defunctoru' : Anno Dom : 1679.

Jone Hoickles buried Decem : 26 79 and an aff affidavit delivered Decem : 29 79.
Tho : Watson buried Janu : 23 and an affidavit delivered Janu : 28 1679.
Isabell Franland buried March 3th and an affidavit delivered March 7th 1679.
Margret the daughter of Christo : Lambert buried March 6th & an affidavit delivered March 10th 1679.

Nomina defunctoru' Año Dom : 1680.

Ann Frankland buried Aprill 2th & an affidavit delivered Aprill 17th 1680.
Fransis Hewit buried Augus 24th 1680 and an Affidavit delivered Augus 30 1680.
Christoph : Constantine buried Septem : 27th day 1680 and an Affidavit delivered Octo 1th day 1680.
Susanna the daughter of Samuell Tennant of Chappellhouse was buried in Lining Octo : 7th day 1680 and the Fine payd and delivered to ye poore according to ye late Act.
An Infant child of Henry Leylands buried Octo : 14th 1680 and an Affidavit delivered Octo : 20th day.
James Tennant of Conistonn was buried Febru : 10th day 1680 and an Affidavit delivered Feb : 15th

Nomina bapt : 1680.

Margt and Susanna the daughters of Samuell Tennant of Chappellhouse bap : August 12th 1680.
Laurence the sonn of Cuth : Holiday bap : Aug : 15th 1680.
James the sonn of Charles Hars bap : Janu : 1680.

vltimo die Martij. Anno R. Rs. Caroli Secundi Nunc Angliæ ... .. [B fol. 1 r. Annoq. Dom: 1679.

Be it hereby then remembred and recorded for p'uentinge all further disputes and differrence that at anie time may or shall happen amongst anie the Parissioners and Inhabitants w^th^in the Parish of Burnsall concerninge the repaireinge & vpholdinge the Parish Church of Burnsall afforesaid and other charges Incident by law to be imposed vpon the said Parish, It is therefore hereby fullye and absolutelye agreed and concluded vpon and amongst the p'sent officers Church wardens and overseers of . . . said Parish together by and w^th^ the aduice p'uitie and con . . . . of diuers of the principall men of the said Parish whose . . . . are herevnto subscribed.

1^st^ That of right continued by antient custom that the Parson of the said Parish maintaine decentlie and suffitientlye vphold the Chancell of the said Church w^th^ the Roofe windowes walls and flore, w^th^in and w^th^out.

2^lie^ That the townes called and reputed the low p'te of the said Parish, That is to say Burnsall cum Thorpe, Hartlinton Woodhowse and Apletreeweicke shall and Will at all times hereafter well and suffitientlie maintaine vphold & repaire, All the Steeplehowse together w^th^ the Bells, Bell ropes, & Clockes, And whatsoeuer therevnto doth shall or may belonge.

3^lie^ That the townes and places abouenamed and called the low p'te of the Parish shall well & decentlie make good and vphold all the Stalls and Seaats w^th^in the bodie of the Said Parish Church.

4^lie^ That for and in regard of the Roofe both inside & Outside over the bodie of the said Church as Alsoe the Walls of the bodie of y^e^ Church both inside and outside together w^th^ the Windowes therevnto belonginge, shall be maintained and vpholden as followeth vidz^t^ the Parish according to antient custom beinge diuided into fowre quarters for payinge the lame Souldjers gald The Lower p'te of the Parish shall according to the number of their howses pay for euerie howse two pence in regard of the benefitte they haue by their seats, whereas the rest of the said Parish shall but pay three halfepence a howse but the said sumes of twopence and three halfepence a house shall be doubled tribled and further augmented as Just cause, and necessitie for the repaire or beautificinge the bodie of y^e^ said Church or flaginge the Allies shall require. And that the Church officers for the whole Parish shall at all times hereafter haue there voats in the Festinge of all such work as shall at anie time belonge to the roofe of the said Church its bodie walls windowes and Allies thereof.

That the Communion Booke and Church bible shall be prouided at the Charge of the whole Parishe accordinge to the rates abouesaid for the said Church of Burnsall.

That the said Parish Church, Coniston Parochiall Chappell and Rilston Parochiall Chappell shall by there seuerall Churchwardens be p'uided for of bread and wine in order to the distributinge and receiueinge of the Sacram^te^ of the Supper of o^r^ blessed lord and Sauiou^r^

Jesus Christ euerie of them beinge onelie accomptable w^th^in themselues for the same.

[B fol. 1 v.

That Foxe heads &c be paid for w^th^in each Constablerie where they weare Kild and not put into the generall accompt of the Parish in regard of the Largnesse thereof the inhabitants haue beene abused and Cheated as by seuerall haue beene obserued.

Chr : Lancaster
Rect of y^e^ one Medit : of Burnsall
Cuth : Wade
Tho : Craven
Nicholas Blackburne
Nicolas Blackborne Junr.
Chr : Dawson
John Layland
Edward Thompson
Tho : Hitching
Thomas Anderson

---

John Garforth
Tho : Aireton
Willya' West
Michaell Taileforth
William Batty marke ×
William Hodgeson marke × } Churchwardens.
George broughton
Humfra Bland
William Paget marke P.
Robert Ellis marke R

Anno Dom. 1701 Received of Dani : Preston y^e^ sum of 11^s^ out of this sum of this same yeare y^e^ sum of 9^s^ 6^d^ to Kilnsey poore &c to Conistones poore y^e^ sum of 6^s^ 6^d^

[B fol. 2 r.

An : Domini 1686 Aprill the 26.

A True & perfect Clause of y^e^ last will & Testament of John Hartley of Kilnsay belonging to owre poore &c.

And provided also & upon Condition that hee the said Henery Motley his executores Administratores & Assignes shall likewise well & truly pay to the poore people of the Township of Conistone in Kettlewelldale & Kilnsay aforesaid all such moneyes as shall be raised out of the rents & profits of all my said Lease Lands Situate within Bordley aforesaid yearly after my death dureing the Continuance of all my terme & termes of yeares therein upon the feast day of St : Thomas the Appostle being the Twenty first day of December except three shillings thereof yearely which I doe hereby limit & Appoint shall be paid yearely out of the same upon S^t^ Thomas day aforesaid to the three daughters now living of Anthony Procter of Bordley aforesaid viz : every one twelve pence A piece for soe many yeares after my death of the said Lease as they shall happen to live & it is my Will & minde that all the remainder of such moneyes as shall be yearly raised out of the said rents & profitts of my Lease Lands within Bordley aforesaid shall be yearely distributed at the discression of the Curate & Overseers of the Poore for the time being within Conistone & Kilnsay aforesaid; And Provided likewise & upon Condition that if Default be made in payment of such said moneyes as shall be raised out of the rents & profitts of my said Lease Lands Sittuate within Bordley aforesaid to be distributed yearely to the poore as aforesaid that then it shall & may be Lawfull to & for the Overseers of the poore of Conistone & Kilnsay aforesaid for the time being to enter into & enjoy the said Lease Lands within Bordley aforesaid & set let & dispose of the same & receive & distribute the rents & profitts thereof at the discression of the said Curate there for the time being amongst the said poore according to my true meaning in & by this my last Will & Testament declared.

An Account what grassing there is in the Mastilles belonging to oure poore & first

An: Dom: 1684 Three whole gates. An: Dom: 1685 Fower whole gates. An: Dom: 1686 Fower whole gates. Tow being allwayes stinted at Mid Aprill & A third allwayes at the twenty fourth of May & when A fourth Gate doth happen it is Stinted the first of May except every third yeare wherein it is Stinted the Twenty fourth day of May & in every of these years pasturage for an Ewe & A Lambe over & above these gates & at the eight day of June every yeare these doth come in Seaven Lambe gates over & above all that is here before reaconed.

[B fol. 3 r.

A true Register of All Christnings Marriages & Burialls that have been at y^e^ Perociall Chappell at Conistone within the Parrish of Burnsall since the beginning of the yeare of oure Lord God An: Dom: 1682.

Nomina Sponsalium An: Dom 1682.

Will: Sarjantson & Frances Wade mar: february the 8.

Nomina Bapti: eodem anno /82.

Will: the son of Tho: Layland de Chappellhouse paptiz: May th. 4.
Margret y^e^ daughter of Jo: Hasledine of Kil: bap: November th. 12.
Blencow y^e^ son of Sam: Tenãnt de Chappellhouse bap: December th. 28.
Henery y^e^ son of Rich. Challinhouse de Conistone bap: February th. 4.

Nomina defunctor: eod' anno /82 & aflid: deliv'ed according to alate statute & act made & intitled for burying in woollen.

Henery Constantine of Conistone buried Aprill th. 29.
Margret y^e^ Daughter of Rich^d^ Wigglesworth de Conis: buri: May th. 6.
An Infant Child of Will' Tod de Conistone buried June th. 18.
Genet y^e^ daughter of Joh: Layland seni' de Conis' buri: August th. 20.
Jonathan y^e^ son of Joh: Hewit de Conis: buri: February th. 3.
Richard Frankland de Conistone buri: February th. 21.
Thomas Aerton buried in linnen March th. 3.

Nomina bapti. An. Dom. 1683.

Hellen $y^e$ daughter of Henery Robbinson bapti : October th. 28.
An : $y^e$ daughter of Rich[d] Wigglesworth de Conist : bapti : December th. 2.
Hanna $y^e$ daughter of Thomas Layland de Chappell' bap : December th. 23.

Nomina defunctor : eodem anno & affidavits deliv[r]ed according to alate Act made & intitled for burying in woollen.

John Hartley buried in Linnen Aprill th. 16.
John Horner de Conistone buried Aprill th. 19.
An : the Wife of Richard Wigglesworth de Conist : buri : Decem' th. 2.
Richard Constantine de Conistone buried March th. 24.

Nomina bapti : An : Dom : 1684.

John $y^e$ son of Jam : Sidgeweeke bapti : March th. 30.
Margret the daughter of Jo : Constantine de Conist : bap : Aprill th. 6.
Thomas $y^e$ son of Hen : Layland de Conistone bap : May th. 4.
Joseph $y^e$ son of Tho : Ibbotson de Kiln : pap : August th. 10.
Richard $y^e$ son of Tho : Constantine de Conist : bap : August th. 8.
Alice $y^e$ daughter of Rich[d] Challinhouse de Conist : bap : October th. 21.
William $y^e$ son of Jo : Winser de Conist : bap : November th. 10.
Elizabeth $y^e$ daughter of Tho : Frankland de Conist : bap : March th. 23.

Nomina defunctor : eodem anno & affidavits deliver : according to A late Act made & intitled for burying in wollen.

Blencow $y^e$ son of Sam : Tenānt de Chappell : buri : May th. 19.
M[r] William Tenānt de Chappellhouse buri : June th. 29.
Dorathy Frankland de Conist' buri : August th. 26.
Robert Constantine de Conist : buri : October th. 10.
Anne Ward de Kilnsay buried November th. 12.
Richard Darbieshire buried December th. 14.
George Frankland de Conistone buri : January th. 7.

Nomina Sponsalium An : Dom : 1685.

John Sariantson & Elizabeth Horner Widdow married November th. 22.

Nomina Bapti' eodem anno.

Margret $y^e$ daughter of Sam : Tenānt de Chap : bap : June th. 18.
William $y^e$ son of John Hosledine de Kiln : bap : July th. 19.
George $y^e$ Son of Hen : Robbinson de Kiln : bap : January th. 11.
Rich : $y^e$ son of Will : Tod de Conist : bap : February th. 28.
John $y^e$ son of Tho : Layland de Chapp : bap : February th. 28.

Nomina defunctor : eodem anno & Affidavits deliv[r]ed according to A late Act made & intitled for burying in woollen.

Francis $y^e$ son of Rich : Battie de Conist : buri : Aprill the 3.
Will : West senior de Conistone buried May th. 7.
Leonard Geldart de Conistone buried May th. 21.
Elizabeth $y^e$ daughter of Tho : Frankland de Conist : buri : June th. 8.

Anne y^e^ daughter of Rich : Wigglesworth de Conist : buri : November th. 19.
Margret y^e^ wife of John Layland senior de Conist : buri : March th. 5.
Will : Tod senior of Conistone buried March th. 11.

Nomina sponsaliu' anno domi' 1686.

George Metcalfe & Genitt Constantine of Kilnsay married May y^e^ 25^th^

Nomina defunctoru' eode' anno.

George y^e^ sonn of Henry Robinson of Kilnsay buried May y^e^ 9^th^
Ann ye wife of Rich : Batty buried July y^e^ 6^th^
John Layland senor of Conistone buried July y^e^ 16^th^
Ann y^e^ daughter of John Hebdin of Coniston buried february y^e^ 1^th^
Joseph y^e^ somne of Tho : Ibbottson of Kilnsay buried March y^e^ 18^th^

Nomina pueror' eodem anno.

Willia' y^e^ sonn of Chris : Mallison of Coniston bap : July y^e^ 30^th^
James y^e^ sonn of James Sidgwicke bap : August y^e^ 1^th^
Tho : y^e^ son of Daniell Preston bap : octb^r^ y^e^ 21^th^ 86. [B fol. 3 v.
Marg : y^e^ daugh : of Tho : Frankland of Coniston bap : deb^r^ y^e^ 9^th^
Henry y^e^ son of John Coniston of Coniston bap : deceb^r^ y^e^ 26^th^
Jenitt y^e^ daug : of John Midlbrough of Coniston bap : Jan : y^e^ 16^th^
John y^e^ sonn of Sam : Tennant of Chappelhouse bap : febr : y^e^ 8^th^

Nomina Sponsaliu' Anno domi' 1687.

Martin Binks & Isabell Franckland of Conis : maried May y^e^ 18^th^

Nomina puer : eodem Anno.

Willia' y^e^ sonn of Tho : Constant : of Coniston bap : May y^e^ 1^th^ 87.
James y^e^ sonn of Henry Robinson bap : August y^e^ 7^th^ 87.
John y^e^ sonn of John Dixon of Bordley bap : Dece : y^e^ 4^th^ 87.
Henry y^e^ sonn of Tho : Layland bap : feb : y^e^ 26^th^ 87.

Ann Nomina defunct' eodem anno.

John y^e^ sonn of John Winder of Kilnsay buri : May y^e^ 21^th^ 87.
John Sidgswicke of Kilnsay buried septenb^r^ y^e^ 16^th^ 87.
Will : y^e^ sonn of Tho : Constantine buried deceb^r^ y^e^ 25^th^ 87.
Tho : Hebdin of Coniston buried feb : y^e^ 15^th^ 87.

Nomina Sponsaliu' Anno domi' 1688.

Chris Ibbottson of Kettlwell & Ellin Batty daug : of Rich : Batty Coni : mar : June y^e^ [22 day of June 1688].

Nomina pueroru' eodem Anno.

Ann y^e^ daug : of Chris : Brodbelt of Kilnsay bap : Aprill y^e^ 8^th^
Elizabeth y^e^ daug : of Chris : Lambert Junor bap : Aprill y^e^ 17^th^
Ann y^e^ daug : of Rich : Challinghouse of Coniston bap : Ap : y^e^ 19^th^
Robert y^e^ sonn of Rich : Wiglsworth Coniston bap : June y^e^ 28^th^
John y^e^ sonn of Daniell Preston bap : Sep : y^e^ 20^th^
John y^e^ sonn of Jonathan Hughs bap : Janu : y^e^ 27^th^

nomina defunct' eodem anno.

Tho : Lonsdale Kilnsay buried May y^e^ 1^th^ 88.
Jane Constantine of Conist : buried May y^e^ 13^th^
George Bramham of Conist : buried May y^e^ 14^th^

Henry $y^e$ son of Tho : Layland de Chappelhouse buried July $y^e$ $27^{th}$
Mary $y^e$ daug : of Ho : Hewitt de Conist : buried August $y^e$ $30^{th}$
Ann $y^e$ daug : of Rich : Challinghouse Conist : bur : Sept : $y^e$ $10^{th}$
Cuth : Wade Esquire buried in Linnen Sep : $y^e$ $11^{th}$ 88.
Fran : Wattson buri : $Noveb^r$ $y^e$ $1^{th}$
Elizabeth Airton of Scarthcoate buried $Noveb^r$ $y^e$ $18^{th}$

Nomina puero : Anno domi' 1689.

Henry $y^e$ son of Tho : Constant : Conist : bap : Aprill $y^e$ $10^{th}$
Robert $y^e$ son of John Winser bap : May $y^e$ $10^{th}$
Jonathan $y^e$ son of Tho : Hardicar : bap : Sep : $y^e$ $1^{th}$
John $y^e$ sonn of Tho : Frankland bap : Sep : $y^e$ $15^{th}$
Susanna $y^e$ daug : of Sam : Tennant bap : octo : $y^e$ $1^{th}$
Rich : $y^e$ sonn of Tho : Layland Chapelhouse bap : oct : $y^e$ $3^{th}$
Will : $y^e$ sonn of James Sidgswick bap : $Octb^r$ $y^e$ $6^{th}$
Eliz : $y^e$ daug : of John Constant : Conis : bap : Nove : $y^e$ $13^{th}$
Margrett : $y^e$ daug : of Chris : Lambert Junor bap : January $y^e$ $9^{th}$ 89.

Nomina defunct' : eodem anno 89.

Peter $y^e$ sonn of Margret Hewitt buri : May $y^e$ $4^{th}$
Robert $y^e$ sonn of John Winser buri : May $y^e$ $11^{th}$
Rich : $y^e$ sonn of Tho : Layland Chapelhouse buri : Octo : $y^e$ $5^{th}$
John $y^e$ sonn of Tho : Frankland buried Octo : $y^e$ $6^{th}$
Frances $y^e$ wife of John Layland buried $decemb^r$ $y^e$ $25^{th}$ 89.
John Rogers of Kilnsay buried Janu : $y^e$ $6^{th}$ 89.

Nomina pueror' Anno Domi' 1690.

Thomasin $y^e$ daug : of Tho : Constantine Conist : bap : May $y^e$ $25^{th}$
Tho : $y^e$ sonn of Henry Robinson bap : June $y^e$ $15^{th}$
Ann $y^e$ daug : of Tho : Layland Chapelhouse bap : $Novemb^r$ $y^e$ $13^{th}$
Jane $y^e$ daug : of Tho : frankland bap : $decemb^r$ $y^e$ $4^{th}$
Tho : $y^e$ sonn of Rich : Wiglsworth bap : Febr : $y^e$ $18^{th}$

Nomina defunct : eodem anno 90.

Genitt Collinson of Coniston buried Aprill $y^e$ $9^{th}$
an Infant Child of Tho : Constantine bur : May $y^e$ $25^{th}$
Thomasin $y^e$ daug : of Tho : Constantine buried June $y^e$ $6^{th}$
Ann Rogers of Kilnsay bur : feb : $y^e$ $2^{th}$ 1690.

Nomina Sponsaliu' Anno Dom' 1691. [B fol. 4 r.

Robert Fell & Margrett Frankland maried January $y^e$ $7^{th}$ 91.

nomina pueroru' eodem Anno.

Mary $y^e$ daug : of Chris : Lambert Jun : bap : Aprill $y^e$ $1^{th}$
Daniell $y^e$ sonn of Daniell Preston bap : Apr : $y^e$ $22^{th}$
Jonathan $y^e$ sonn of Jonathan Hughes bap : Sep : $y^e$ $26^{th}$
Frances $y^e$ daughter of Will : Hewitt bap : $decemb^r$ $y^e$ $8^{th}$

Nomina defunct' : eodem anno.

Roger Frankland of Coniston buried Aprill $y^e$ $5^{th}$
Elizab : Constantine of Conis : buried $Noveb^r$ $y^e$ $14^{th}$ 1691.

Nomina bapti : Anno Dom' 1692.

Genitt $y^e$ daughter of Robert Mitton bap : May $y^e$ $2^d$ 1692.
Isabell $y^e$ daughter of John Constantine bap : June $y^e$ 20 1692.

Mary y[e] daughter of John Newsom of Coniston bap: Septemb[r] y[e] 4[th] 92.
Chris: y[e] sonn of Chris: Lambert bap: Decemb[r] y[e] 10[th] 92.
Rebecca y[e] daughter of Cuth: Wade bap: Decemb[r] y[e] 14[th] 92.
Willia' y[e] sonn of Rich: Wiglsworth bap: Decemb[r] y[e] 28 92.
Elizabeth y[e] daughter of Tho: Johnson bap: January y[e] 1[th] 92.
Henry y[e] sonn of Tho: Layland bap: February 28[th] 92.

Nomina Defunctoru' eodem Anno 92.

Robert Mitton of Kilnsay buried March y[e] 11[th] Anno Dom: 92.
Tho: Ibbottson buried June y[e] 2[d] 92.
Ed: Hartley buried June y[e] 19[th] 92.
John Constantine of Coniston buried August y[e] 20[th] 92.
Isabell y[e] daughter of Francis Constantine buried August y[e] 22[d] 92.
Frances Sidgwick of Kilnsay buried October y[e] 13[th] 92.
Margrett Bramham buried Decemb[r] 1[th] 92.
Mr Tho: Warde buried March y[e] 21[th] 92.

Nomina Sponsaliu' 92.

Rich: Constantine of Coniston & Ellin Halton maried Febru: y[e] 24[th] 92.

Nomina Bap: Anno Dom: 1693.

Robert y[e] sonn of Rich: Constantine Jun[r] bap June y[e] 22[d] 93.
Frances y[e] daughter of James Sidgwick bap June y[e] 28[th] 93.
Rich: y[e] sonn of John Ellis Coniston bap: August y[e] 28[th] 93.
Cuth: Wade y[e] sonn of Cuth: Wade bap: Novemb[r] y[e] 14[th] 93.
Margrett y[e] daughter of Tho: Knowles bap: February y[e] 4[th] 93.
Roger y[e] sonn of Daniell Preston bap: February y[e] 19[th] 93.

Nomina Defunct' eodem Anno.

Chris: Settle of Coniston buried Septemb[r] y[e] 9[th] 93.
M[r] Cuth: Wade buried January y[e] 9[th] 93.

Nomina Sponsalium eodem Anno.

Tho: Jackson of Linton & Jane Kidd was maried July 16[th] 93.

Nomina bap: Anno Domi' 1694.

Tho: y[e] sonn of John Newsom bap: July y[e] 3[d] 94.
Eliz: y[e] daughter of Will: Hewitt bap: Sep: 30[th] 94.
Eliz: y[e] daughter of John Ellis bap: January 22[d] 94.
Eliz: y[e] daughter of Rich: Constantine Ju[r] bap: february 24[th] 94.

Nomina Defuncto: eodem anno.

John y[e] sonn of Chris: Mallison buri: June 29[th] 94.
Tho: y[e] sonn of John Newsom buri: July 13[th] 94.
John y[e] sonn of Chris: Petty buri: January 25[th] 94.
Mary Layland buri: March y[e] 3[d] 94.
John Tunsdill buri: March y[e] 17[th] 94.

Nomina Bap 1695.

Jonathan y[e] son of Tho: Constantine bap May 20[th] 95.
John y[e] sonn of Chris: Lambert bap Sep: 1[th] 95.
John y[e] sonn of John Newsom bap octob[r] 27[th] 95.
Emm y[e] Daug: of Tho: Knowles bap Janu: 12[th] 95.
George y[e] sonn of James Sidgwick bap March 24[th] 95.

Nomina Sponsalium eodem anno.

Will: Lawson & Dorothy Ibbottson maried Aprill 22d 95.

Nomina Defunct: eodem Anno.

An Infant child of George Horner buri: Aprill 1th 95.
Katharine ye Daughter of Tho: Carr buri: May ye 5th 95.
Agnes ye Wife of John Wilkinson buried June ye 3d 95. [B fol. 4 v.
Agnes ye Daughter of John Hesleton buri: July ye 6th 95.
Isabell ye Daughter of Tho: Layland buri: Sep: 14th 95.
An Infant child of Tho: Frankland buri: Octo: 30th 95.
Tho: ye sonn of John Shacklton buri: Nove: 3d 95.
An Infant child of John Shacklton buri Novem: 22d 95.
Ann ye wife of John Shackleton buri Novembr 27th 95.
John ye sonn of Chris Lambert Jur bur: March 8th 95.

Nomina defunctoru' et Sponsaliu' et baptiz' 1696.

Hannah ye wife of Will: Hewitt buried January ye 20th 96.
Florence Hewitt of Coniston bur: January ye 29th 96.
Will: Todd of Coniston bur: february ye 6th 96.
*Robert Mallison
Robert Malham of Coniston buri: february ye 21th 96.
John Leyland buried february ye 25th 96.
Isabell Hesleton bur: July ye 13th 96.
Ann Winder buri: August ye 8th 96.
Tho: Constantine bur: Septembr ye 15th 96.

Nomina Sponsaliu' eodem Anno 96.

John Winder & Elizabeth Mophitt marri: feb: ye 6th 1696.

Nomina Baptizan': eodem anno 1696.

John ye sonn of George Horner bapt: August ye 16th 1696.
Rich: ye sonn of Daniell Preston bapt: Septembr 27th 96.
Anthony ye sonn of Tho: Johnson Bapt: March 7th 96.

Nomina Sponsiu' et Defunct': et Baptizand: 1697.

Nomina Sponsaliu' eodem anno 1697.

Tho: Coates of Kettlwell & Agnes Winser of Coniston marri: Aprill 4th

Nomina Baptiz: eodem anno 1697.

Tho: ye sonn of Rich: Constantine Junr bap: Aprill 15th 97.
Frances ye daughter of Tho: Franckland bap: Oct: 11th 97.
John ye sonn of John Winder bap: January ye 12th 97.
George ye sonn of Tho: Knowles bap: Jan: 30th 97.
Robert ye sonn of Tho: Stoney bap: February 20th 97.
Will: ye sonn of Tho: Settle bap: March ye 6th 97.

Nomina defunct: eodem anno 1697.

Tho: ye sonn of Rich: Constantine buried Aprill 17th 97.
Antho: Warde of North Coate buri: May ye 24th 97.
John Wilkinson buri: August ye 25th 97.
George ye sonn of James Sidgswick bur: octo: 25th 97.
Frances ye daug: of Tho: Franckland bur: octo: 31th 97.

---

* This entry has been obliterated.

Nomina defunctoru' Anno Dom' 1698.

William y$^{e}$ sonn of John Windser bur : Aprill y$^{e}$ 12$^{th}$ 98.
Chris : Dodsworth of Coniston bur : Aprill y$^{e}$ 16 98.
George y$^{e}$ sonn of Tho : Knowles bur : Aprill 29 98.
Chris : Halliday y$^{e}$ sonn of Cuth Halliday bur : March 14 98.
Chris : Broadbelt of Kilnsay bur : May y$^{e}$ 5$^{th}$ 98.
Jane Halliday of Kilnsay bur : August y$^{e}$ 4$^{th}$ 98.
Genitt y$^{e}$ wife of John Broadbelt bur : Nov : 20$^{th}$ 98.
John Midlebrook buried feb : y$^{e}$ 14$^{th}$ 98.

Nomina bap : eodem Anno.

Alice y$^{e}$ daughter of Rich : Constantine Jun$^{d}$ bap : Aprill 22$^{d}$ 98.
John y$^{e}$ sonn of Chris : Lambert bap : June y$^{e}$ 16$^{th}$ 98.
Chris : y$^{e}$ sonn of Chris : Petty bap : Sep : y$^{e}$ 14$^{th}$ 98.
Robert y$^{e}$ sonn of John Ellis bap : Nov 30$^{th}$ 98.

Nomina Sponsalium eodem anno.

Ed : Hesleton & Jane Hodgson mari : Decemb$^{r}$ 7$^{th}$ 98.
Tho : Rathmill & Jane Deane mari : Janu : 15$^{th}$ 98.

Nomina Defunctoru' Anno Dom' 1699. [B fol. 5 r.

Elizabeth the wife of Chris : Lambert sen$^{r}$ buri : Aprill y$^{e}$ 2$^{d}$ 99.
Henry Leyland of Coniston buri : Aprill the 5$^{th}$ 99.
Bernerd y$^{e}$ sonn of Daniell Preston buri : June y$^{e}$ 13$^{th}$ 99.

Nomina bapti : eodem anno.

Bernerd y$^{e}$ sonn of Daniell Preston bap : Aprill 3$^{d}$ 99.
Anne y$^{e}$ daughter of Tho : Knowles bap : Aprill y$^{e}$ 30$^{th}$ 99
George y$^{e}$ sonn of James Sidgswick bap July y$^{e}$ 9$^{th}$ 99.
Anne the daughter of John Holmes of Kilnsay bap : Oct : y$^{e}$ 17$^{th}$ 99.
Margrett y$^{e}$ daughter of Tho : Stoney of Con : bap : feb : y$^{e}$ 4$^{th}$ 99.
Agnes the daughter of Chris : Lambert bap : March 19$^{th}$ 99.
Jane y$^{e}$ daughter of John Hebden Jun$^{r}$ of Con : bap : March 24 99.

Nomina defunct : et bap : et sponsaliu' Anno dom : 1700.

Tho : y$^{e}$ sonn of John Hebden of Con : buri : Aprill 3$^{d}$ 1700.
Alice y$^{e}$ wife of Tho : Constantine of Con : buri : Aprill y$^{e}$ 5$^{th}$ 1700.
Margrett y$^{e}$ daughter of George fawcitt of Con : bap : Aprill 11$^{th}$ 1700.
Elizabeth West of Coniston bur May y$^{e}$ 9$^{th}$ 1700.
John y$^{e}$ sonn of Jane Leyland buri June y$^{e}$ 1$^{th}$ 1700.
Alice y$^{e}$ wife of George Fawcitt of Con bur June y$^{e}$ 2$^{d}$ 1700.
Mary y$^{e}$ daughter of Dan : Preston bap : June y$^{e}$ 5$^{th}$ 1700.
Michill Settle of Coniston bur July y$^{e}$ 6$^{th}$ 1700.
Elizabeth y$^{e}$ wife of Jo : Hebden Coni bur August 8$^{th}$ 1700.
Tho : Constantine de Con : bur : August y$^{e}$ 12$^{th}$ 1700.
Robert y$^{e}$ sonn of Will : Slinger bap : Decem : y$^{e}$ 5$^{th}$ 1700.
James y$^{e}$ sonn of Jo : Tennant of Conisto : bap : Janua : 5$^{th}$ 1700.
Christiana y$^{e}$ daughter of Tho : Johnson de Con. bap Jan y$^{e}$ 1$^{th}$ 1700.
Mary y$^{e}$ daug : of Chris : Petty de Kilnsay bap Jan y$^{e}$ 5$^{th}$ 1700.
Jane y$^{e}$ daug : of John Hebden jun$^{r}$ de Con : buri : Feb : 2$^{d}$ 1700.
Mary y$^{e}$ daug : of Chris : Petty Kiln : buri March 22$^{d}$ 1700.

Nomina bap: et defunct: et Sponsa: Anno Dom: 1701.

Henry y^e^ sonn of Will: Hewitt borne Aprill 2^d^—This putt in y^e^ publick Register att y^e^ desire of his Father & bap in y^e^ same Aprill y^e^ 22^d^ 1701.
Mary y^e^ daug of Jona: Hughes de Kiln: bap Ap: 27^th^ 1701.
Joseph y^e^ son of Edward Heseltine bap Agust: 1.
Joan y^e^ Daughter of W^m^ Hewit born Feb y^e^ 28 1703.
Thomas y^e^ son of John Hebdin born June 14.
William y^e^ son of Francis Layland bap: Sep: 29 —03.
George the son of Th^os^ Jonson Bab^d^ Sep^r^ 30^th^ —03.
Richard Wigglesworth buried March y^e^ 8 — 03.

Nomina sponsalium.

Georg Horner married Sep: y^e^ 26 1703.

Bapt: 1708. [B fol. 5 v.

W^m^ the Son of George Horner Bap: May 16^th^
Mary y^e^ Daughter of W^m^ Hewit Bap: July 4^th^
Rob^t^ the Son of Rob^t^ Hardcastle Bap: July 11^th^
Jane the Daughter of George Faucett Bap: July 23.
Jane y^e^ Daughter of Tho: Leyland Bap: Sep 26.
Anne the Daughter of John Ellis Bap: Dec: 8^th^
Willyam the Son of William Slinger Baptised feb ^th^ 6.

Sepulti 1708.

Cath: the Wife of Hen: Ibbotson Bur: June 8^th^
Mary Arton Widdow Buried June 23^d^
John Hebdon sen^r^ Buried Decemb^r^ 4^th^

1709.

Margret the doughter of John hebden bap: aprell ^th^ 3.
Thomas the sun of tho ivnson babtised June the ninten.
M. Susaney the dauter of John tenand bap June the 20—1.
Eada the douter of John tenent baptised June the 20—6.
Ann the of rob malinson baptised.
Rob^t^ Slinger buried 15 day of Jencyw'
Thom^m^: Cnoles bured febery the 26—0.
Ann the douter of tho pulman bured 1710.

Nuptiæ.

Ric. Blacburne and Dickinson Dec 8^th^
Tho. Stoney

1703. [B fol. 6 r.

Tho: y^e^ Son of John Hebdin Bap june y^e^ 27^d^
Will y^e^ Sun of francis Lelend Bap Sep y^e^ 29^d^
Richard y^e^ Sun of Will^m^ Slinger Bap: octob^r^ y^e^ 17^d^
Margret y^e^ Daught^r^ of Tho: Setle Bap: january y^e^ 13.
Jane Leland Buried Augus y^e^ 12^d^
Jane y^e^ Daught^r^ of Will Huit Buried janury y^e^ 8^d^

1704.

The 9^th^ day of Aprill James y^e^ sonne of Will: Hewitt baptised.

May y^e^ 15th Margarett y^e^ doughter of Tho Settle buried.
Cicely y^e^ wife of Tho : Frankland buried October y^e^ second.
Richard y^e^ sonne of george Horner baptised Nouember y^e^ first.
Anne y^e^ daughter of Will : Frankeland buried March y^e^ 24th

1705.

John Hesleton buried Aprill the 15th

[Adhuc Ex. p. S.B.]

George the sun of Georg Facit Bap. March the 11th
Dorithy y^e^ daughter of John Tennant Bap : July y^e^ 8d
Alis y^e^ wife of Robert Slinger was buried Septeber 30d
Janet y^e^ daughter of Robert Malingson was Bap : Oct 1d
W^m^ Holiday was buried Januar' : y^e^ 20 1705.
Mary y^e^ Wife of Anth : Allen was buried Feb : y^e^ 12.

Ann' 1706.

Eada y^e^ Wife of James Tennant was buried Ap : 6th 1706.
Rich : y^e^ Son of Daniell Preston was buried Aprill 23d 1706.

Nomina Bapt :

Henry y^e^ Son of John Hebden baptized May 12th 1706.
Alice y^e^ Daughter of W^m^ Slinger Baptiz'd July 27th —06.
Henry y^e^ Son of Thomas Leyland Bap : May 19th —06.
Jane (?) y^e^ Daughter of W^m^ Hewitt Bap : May 26th —06.
Margrett the Daughter of Jo^n^ Tenn^t^ Baptiz'd Feb^r^ 2d $170\frac{6}{7}$

Nomina Defuncto^r^

Robert Fell buried Febur' the 6th $170\frac{6}{7}$.
Anne Settle buried Janua' 16th $170\frac{7}{8}$.
Anne the Daughter of W^m^ Frankland buried feb' the first $170\frac{7}{8}$.
Margt the Wife of Jo^n^ Hebden buried feb' 15th $170\frac{7}{8}$.
M^rs^ Jane Ratcliffe Interred in the Chappell of Coniston being an hospitall Woman February the 25th in ye year $170\frac{7}{8}$.

Nomina Sponsalium Anno 1707.

Tho : Stoney & Fran : Widdowes Married Decemb^r^ the 15th 1707.

Nomina Bap :

John the Son of John Sledd Bap feb^r^ 8th $170\frac{7}{8}$.
Dorothy the Daugh ' of M^r^ Jo^n^ Tenn^t^ bap : Feb : 15 $170\frac{7}{8}$.
Be it hereby Remembred that a son of John Holmes of Kilnsey Baptised Aug y^e^ 17th
Christopher y^e^ son of Robt Maulison of Conistone baptized Octob^r^ 31.

Nomina Sepultorum añ : 1710. [B fol. 6 v.

Richard Todd buried Nov^r^ 1710.
Eliz : Wigglesworth buried March 21 $17\frac{10}{11}$.

Nomina Bapt : 1710.

Rob^t^ the Son of Tho : Pulman Bap : Feb : 11th
Charles y^e^ Son of Rich : Abbotson Bap : Feb : 25.
Samuel y^e^ Son of M^r^ John Tenn^t^ Bap : March 7th
Henry y^e^ Son of Rob^t^ Hardcastle Bap : March 11th

Nomina Sepultorum Anñ : 1711.

Jane y$^{e}$ Daughter of Tho : Leyland Buried Ap : 13$^{th}$
Anne y$^{e}$ Wife of M$^{r}$ John Tenn$^{t}$ Buried May 31$^{st}$
Samuel y$^{e}$ Son of M$^{r}$ John Tenn$^{t}$ Buried July 30$^{th}$
Agnes Malison Buried August 9$^{th}$
Margret Buxton Buried January 10$^{th}$
Ann y$^{e}$ Daughter of John Ellis Buried January y$^{e}$ 15$^{th}$
Mary y$^{e}$ Daughter of John Ellis Buried February y$^{e}$ 27$^{th}$

Nomina Baptiz : 1711.

Anne y$^{e}$ Daughter of W$^{m}$ Hewitt Bap : May 13$^{th}$
Mary the daughter of John Ellis Bap : Nov$^{r}$ 11$^{th}$
Henrey Smith & Agnes Greenbank Married Jan : y$^{e}$ 8$^{th}$

Nomina Baptiz : 1712.

Isabel y$^{e}$ Daughter of John Tennant Bapt : june y$^{e}$ 30$^{th}$
Luke y$^{e}$ son of George Horner Bapt : October y$^{e}$ 19$^{th}$
Margret y$^{e}$ Daughter of Rob$^{t}$ Mallyson Bapt 9$^{ber}$ 29$^{th}$
George y$^{e}$ Son of Rob$^{t}$ Hard-castle Bapt March y$^{e}$ 15$^{th}$

Nomina Sepultorum.

Isabel y$^{e}$ Daughter of John Tennant Buried Aug$^{t}$ 10$^{th}$

Nomina Sponsalium.

Rob$^{t}$ Wilkinson and Elizabeth Hewson married Feb : 8$^{th}$

Nomina Bapt : 1713.

John y$^{e}$ Son of John Hebden Bapt : March y$^{e}$ 29$^{th}$
Henry y$^{e}$ Son of John Ellis Bapt : May y$^{e}$ 10$^{th}$
John y$^{e}$ Son of Richard Abbotson Bapt : May 17$^{th}$
Margret y$^{e}$ Daught$^{r}$ of Lowrance Holy-day Bapt July 5$^{th}$

Nomina Sepultorum.

M$^{rs}$ Margret Ward Buried May y$^{e}$ 14$^{th}$
John y$^{e}$ Son of Richard Abbotson Buried July 25$^{th}$
Willi' Mallyson Buried July 28$^{th}$
Rob$^{t}$ Wiglesworth Buried Aug$^{t}$ y$^{e}$ 27$^{th}$

Nomina Sponsalium.

John Eccles & Ellin Robinson Married Ap : y$^{e}$ 14$^{th}$

Nomina Bapt : 1714.

Alice y$^{e}$ Daughter of John Tatterson Bapt. March y$^{e}$ 29$^{th}$
Ellin y$^{e}$ Daughter of Rich$^{d}$ Abbottson Bapt : Aug$^{t}$ 8$^{th}$
Jane y$^{e}$ Daughter of Lowrance Holy-day Bapt 8$^{br}$ 10$^{th}$
Mary y$^{e}$ Daughter of John Tennant Bapt 8$^{br}$ y$^{e}$ 10$^{th}$
Matthew y$^{e}$ son of Wm : Hewitt Bapt : No : y$^{e}$ 21$^{th}$
Elizabeth y$^{e}$ Daughter of George Horner Bapt. Feb : 6$^{th}$
John y$^{e}$ Son of Rob$^{t}$ Mallyson Bapt : Feb : y$^{e}$ 6$^{th}$

Nomina Sepultorum 1714. [B fol. 7 r.

Thomas Frankland Buried June y$^{e}$ 13$^{th}$
Ellin y$^{e}$ Daughter of Rich$^{d}$ Abbotson Buried Augt : y$^{e}$ 22$^{d}$
Elin y$^{e}$ wife of John Winzor Buried Augt : y$^{e}$ 30$^{th}$
William West Buried March y$^{e}$ 13$^{th}$

Nom : Bap : 1715.

W^m son of Jn^o Tenant bap : Aug 27.
Rich^d wiglesworth son of Tho : Wiglesworth bap : Nov^r 27.
Ellen Daught^r of W^m Atkinson bap March 9^th

Nom : Sepult :

Ric : Battie burierd Apr^l 3^d
Agnes Midlesbrough May 13.
Ellen Abbotson Octo^r 27.
Ric : Frankland Decemb^r 8.
Agnes Wiglesworth Decemb^r 11.

Nom : Nup : anno p^rd.

W^m Bastow & Margrett Stockdall married June 10.
Fælix preston & Ann Hawworth married June 11.

Nom' Bap anno 1716.

Ch^r son of Jn^o Tatterson bap May 20.
Martha Daught^r of James Ibbottson bap Decemb^r 16.
Agnes Daught^r of Rob^t Hardcastle bap : Decemb^r 30.
Th : Horner bap : Jan : 27.
W^m Holliday bap : Feb : 3^d
Ric : Mallson bap : Feb : 17.
Alice D^tr of Fælix Preston bap May 6.

Nom' Sepult.

Marg^t Hebden May 11 [Jn^o Hebden May 21].
Alice Layland Aug : 9.
Geo : Frankland Sep^t 5.
Ric : Constantine Jan : 26.
Eliz : Ovington Ap^r 29;

Nom : Nup.

Rob^t Lukas & Jane Wilson mar^d : May 3^d
Ric : Guy & Ellen Pulman mar^d : May 6.
Nicho : Johnson & Ann Broadbelt mar^d May 6.
Law : Wildman & Mary Hardacre Feb : 3^d

Nom : Bap : anno Domi' 1717. [B fol. 7 v.

Eliz : Constantine bap : March 31.
Rich^d Boulton bap : May 14.
Rich^d son of M^r Teñant May 19.
Eliz : Teñant bap Sep^t 22.
Tomisen Atkinson bap : Nov^r 10.
Eliz : Horner bap : Jan : 19.

Nom' Sepult.

Chr Settle buried Decemb^r 10.
George Horner buried March 8.

Nom' : Nup :

Antho : Thompson & Eliz : Mudd married Jan : 13.

Nom : Bap : anno Dom'i 1717.

Eliz : Constantine Daught$^{r}$ of Hen Constantine of Conistone bap March 31 1717.
Ric$^{d}$ Boulton son of Tho : Boulton of Kilnsay bap : May 14 1717.
Rich$^{d}$ Son of M$^{r}$ Jn$^{o}$ Teñant of Chapp' House bap May 19 1717.
Eliz : Daught$^{r}$ of Jn$^{o}$ Teñant of Conistone bap : Sep$^{t}$ 22 1717.
Tomisen Daught$^{r}$ of W$^{m}$ Atkinson bap : Nov$^{r}$ 10 1717.
Eliz Daught$^{r}$ of Jos : Horner of Kilnsey bap : Jan 19 1717.

Nom Sepult.

Chr. Settle of Conistone buried Decemb$^{r}$ 10 1717.
George Horner of Conistone buried March 8 1717.

Nom : Nup :

Anthony Thompson & Eliz : Mudd being three times lawfully published in Burnsalls Chr married Jan : 13 1717.

Nom : Nup : Anno: Dom : 1718. [B fol. 8 r.

Godfrey Horsman of Buerley & Issabell Willson of Kilnsey Married by M$^{r}$ Ricd : Carr Nov$^{r}$ y$^{e}$ 9$^{th}$ Bands thrice published by y$^{e}$ Minist$^{rs}$ of Burnsall & Certified by M$^{r}$ Tho : Furnis of Paitley bridge.
Robert Carlile & Mary Willcock of Kilnsey Married by M$^{r}$ Carr Nov$^{r}$ y$^{e}$ 12$^{th}$ Bands thrice published by y$^{e}$ Minist$^{rs}$ of Burnsall.

Nom : Bap$^{t}$.

Tho : y$^{e}$ Son of Tho : Haworth Lab : Bap$^{d}$ March y$^{e}$ 31$^{th}$
Francis y$^{e}$ Daughter of Hen : Constantine Yeo : Bap$^{t}$ May y$^{e}$ 4$^{th}$
Margrett y$^{e}$ Daughter of John Tattersall Lin : Weaver Bap$^{t}$ May y$^{e}$ 11$^{th}$
Jane y$^{e}$ Daughter of M$^{r}$ John Tennant Gen$^{t}$ Bap$^{t}$ Decemb$^{r}$ y$^{e}$ 14$^{th}$
Mary y$^{e}$ Daug : of James Ibbotson Cordwainer Bap$^{t}$ Feb : y$^{e}$ 15.

Nom : Sepult :

Will : Hewitt Yeo : buried Aug : y$^{e}$ 9$^{th}$
Ric$^{d}$ y$^{e}$ son of Tho : Wigglesworth Yeo : buried Aug$^{t}$ y$^{e}$ 29.
Ric$^{d}$ y$^{e}$ son of M$^{r}$ John Tennant Gen$^{t}$ buried Aug$^{t}$ y$^{e}$ 31.
Ric$^{d}$ Constantine Batchelor buried Jan : y$^{e}$ 27.
Tho : Settle Yeo : buried March y$^{e}$ 15.
Agnes West Widd : buried March y$^{e}$ 21.
Margret y$^{e}$ Dau : of John Tattersall Lin : Weaver buried Octob$^{r}$ y$^{e}$ 15.

Nom Bapt Anno Dom. 1719.

Christopher y$^{e}$ son of Lowrence Holyday of Kilnsey Yeom' Bapt Aprill y$^{e}$ 26.
Mary y$^{e}$ Daug. of Rob$^{t}$ Mallison Tailor Bap$^{t}$ May y$^{e}$ 3$^{d}$
Henry y$^{e}$ Son of Rob$^{t}$ Hardcastle Lab. Bap$^{t}$ June y$^{e}$ 14.
Dorratha y$^{e}$ Daug. of Low. Wildman Lab. Bap November y$^{e}$ 29.
Dorratha y$^{e}$ Daug. of Tho : Bolton Yeom' Bap$^{t}$ December y$^{e}$ 6.
John y$^{e}$ son of Jn$^{o}$ Tattersall Linin weaver Bap : Jan. y$^{e}$ 31.
Margrett y$^{e}$Daug. of Jn$^{o}$ Tattersall aboves$^{d}$ Bap$^{t}$ Jan. y$^{e}$ 31.

Nom : Nup. 1719.

John Watson of Gargrave husbandman & Ann Abbotson of Northcoat Spinster married by M$^{r}$ Pet$^{r}$ Alcock bands thrice published by y$^{e}$ Minist$^{rs}$ of Burnsall & Certified by M$^{r}$ Dodgion Vic$^{r}$ of Gargrave.

John Bowsgill of Arnkclife Miller & Francis Sidgosweek of Kilnsey Spinst^r^ Maried by M^r^ Jn^o^ Alcock bands thrice publish^d^ by y^e^ Minist^rs^ of Burnsall & Certified by M^r^ Tennant Vic^r^ of Arnkclife.

Nom. Sepult. 1719.

Elizabeth y^e^ Wife of Jn^o^ Serjeantson Buried May y^e^ first.
John Tennant of Coniston Yeom' buried May y^e^ 21^st^
Will Frankland of Grislington buried Septemb^r^ y^e^ 22^th^
M^r^ William Tennant of Chapp'house Gent. buried May 3^d^
*a poor man interred at y^e^ expence of y^e^ Tonn of Grislington.

Nom. Bap^t^ Anno Dom. 1720.

Barnard Son of Felix Preston of Kilnsey Blacksmith Bap^t^ Apprill y^e^ tenth 10.
Mary y^e^ Daug of M^r^ Jn^o^ Tennant of Chapp'house Gen^t^ Bap^t^ Aug^t^ y^e^ 22.
Ann y^e^ Daug. of Anth. Allan of Coniston labourour Bap^t^ Aug^t^ y^e^ 28.
Ann y^e^ Daug of Henry Constantine of Coniston Yeom' Bap^t^ Sep^t^ y^e^ 25.

Nom Bap^t^ Anno Dom 1720. [B fol. 8 v.

Sarah y^e^ Daug of Jn^o^ Serjeantson of Coniston Miner Bap^t^ Octob^r^ y^e^ 30^th^
Dorratha y^e^ Daug of Jos. Horner of Coniston Labour: Bap^t^ Decemb^r^ y^e^ 11^th^
Charles y^e^ Son of Will: Atkinson of Coniston husbandman Bap^t^ Feb y^e^ 12^th^
Ann y^e^ Daug^t^ of Will: Atkinson afores^d^ Bap. Feb. 12.

Nom. Nup. 1720.

John Deys of Arnkclif Scoole mast^r^ & Hellen Serjeantson of Chapp'house Serv^t^ married by M^r^ Pet^r^ Alcock bands thrice published by y^e^ Ministers of Burnsall & Certified by M^r^ Tennant Vic^r^ of Arnkclif.

Nom. Sepult. 1720.

Peace Hall of Kilnsey Widd buried Aug^t^ 15^th^
Margrett y^e^ wife of Tho: Johnson of Kilnsey lab^r^ buried Aug^t^ y^e^ 25.
Agnes y^e^ Wife of Rob^t^ Hardcastle of Coniston Min^r^ buried January y^e^ 16.
Charles y^e^ Son of Will. Atkinson of Coniston husband^m^ buried Feb. y^e^ 13.
Ann y^e^ Daug^r^ of Will Atkinson afores^d^ buried Feb. 26^th^

Nom: Nup^t^ Anno Dom. 1721.

Henry Ovinton of Kilnsey Lab: & Agnes Reda of Kilnsey Spinster married decemb^r^ the 30 by M^r^ Carr bands thrice published by the p^r^sons of Burnsall.

Nom: Bap^t^ 1721.

Jane the Daughter of Edward Heseltine of Kilnsey Lab. Bap^t^ June the 11^th^
Elizabeth y^e^ Daughter of John Constantine of Coniston Yeom' Bap^t^ July the 30^th^
Lowrans the Son of Lowrans Holyday of Kilnsey Yeom' Bap^t^ Novemb^r^ y^e^ 26.

* This entry has been carefully erased.

Job the Son of Felix Preston of Kilnsey Blacksmith Bapt Decemb$^{r}$ y$^{e}$ 24.
Henry y$^{e}$ Son of Joseph Skelton of Coniston Lab$^{r}$our Bap$^{t}$ Decemb$^{r}$ y$^{e}$ 30.

Nom. Sepult. 1721.

Christopher Mallison of Coniston Lab. Buried July y$^{e}$ 7$^{th}$
Edward y$^{e}$ Son of Edward Hesletine of Kilnsey Lab. buried Novemb$^{r}$ y$^{e}$ 26.
Elizabeth y$^{e}$ Daughter of John Constantine of Coniston Yeom' buried Decemb$^{r}$ y$^{e}$ 25$^{th}$

Nom : Bap$^{t}$ Anno Dom : 1722.

John y$^{e}$ Son of M$^{r}$ Jn$^{o}$ Tennant of Chapp'house Gent. Bap$^{t}$ Apprill y$^{e}$ 6.
Ann y$^{e}$ Daughter of Will : Atkinson of Northcoat Yeom' Bap$^{t}$ Apprill y$^{e}$ 22.
William y$^{e}$ Son of Rob$^{t}$ Mallison of Coniston Taylor Bap$^{t}$ May y$^{e}$ 20.
Mary y$^{e}$ Daughter of Mary Haworth of Coniston being a Bastard Child Bap$^{t}$ June y$^{e}$ 10.
Agnes y$^{e}$ Daug$^{t}$ of Tho : Boulton of Kilnsey Yeom' Bap$^{t}$ July y$^{e}$ 17.
Margrett y$^{e}$ Daug$^{t}$ of John Constantine of Coniston Yeom' Bap$^{t}$ Decemb$^{r}$ y$^{e}$ 16.
Francis y$^{e}$ Son of Hen : Ovinton of Kilnsey Lab$^{r}$ Bap$^{t}$ Aug$^{t}$ y$^{e}$ 12$^{th}$
Robert y$^{e}$ Son of Jn$^{o}$ Tattersall of Coniston Lining Weaver Bap$^{t}$ Janvary y$^{e}$ 29$^{th}$

Nom. Sepult. 1722. [B fol. 9 r.

Margrett Lupton of Kilnsey Widd buried Aug$^{t}$ y$^{e}$ 3$^{d}$
Jonathan Constantine of Coniston Yeom' buried Novemb$^{r}$ y$^{e}$ 13$^{th}$
Agnes y$^{e}$ Wife of Jonathan Constantine of Coniston Yeom' buried March y$^{e}$ 5$^{th}$

Nom Bap$^{t}$ Anno Dom. 1723.

Elizabeth the Daughter of Eliz Johnson of Kilnsey being a bastard Child Bap$^{t}$ Apprill y$^{e}$ 14$^{th}$
Alice the Daughter of Henry Constantine of Coniston Yeom' Bapt' Apprill the 28$^{th}$
Mary the Daughter of Joseph Horner of Coniston Lab' Bap$^{t}$ June the 23$^{d}$
Rodger the Son of John Serjeantson of Coniston Miner Bap$^{t}$ December the 8$^{th}$
Samuell the Son of John Tennant of Chappelhouse Gen$^{t}$ Bap$^{t}$ February the 7$^{th}$
Robert the Son of James Ibbotson of Kilnsey Cordwainer Bap$^{t}$ Febuary the 9$^{th}$
Cuthbert the Son of Laurence Holyday of Kilnsey Yeom' Bap$^{t}$ March the 1$^{st}$

Nom. Sepul$^{t}$ 1723.

Jennet the Daughter of Edward Hesletine of Kilnsey Miner Buried March the 31$^{st}$
Cuthbert Holyday of Kilnsey Yeom' buried Apprill the 3$^{d}$
John the Son of Thomas Pulman of Coniston Innkeeper buried May the 4$^{th}$

Elizabeth the Wife of Edward Hesletine of Kilnsey Miner buried July the 12th
William the Son of Robert Mallison of Coniston Taylor buried September the 4th
Mary the Daughter of Jos. Horner of Coniston Lab. buried September the 10th
Dorhthy the Daughter of Jos. Horner afores^d buried October the 4th
John Thistlewhite of Kilnsey Innkeeper buried October y^e 14th
Job the Son of Felix Preston of Kilnsey blacksmith buried November the 6th
Thomas the Son of Mary Haworth of Coniston Widd. buried November the 13th
Francis the Son of Henry Ovington of Kilnsey Lab. buried November the 24th
Sarah the Daughter of John Serjantson of Coniston Miner buried February the 2^d
Margrett Fell of Coniston Widd. buried February the 26.
Henry Robinson of Kilnsey paup^r buried March the 2^d

Nom. Sepul^t Anno Dom. 1724.

John Winder of Kilnsey paup^r buried Apprill the 28th
Will: Northall of Kilnsey Lab. buried November the 8.
Mary the Daughter of Mary Haworth of Coniston Widdow buried November the 28th

Nom. Bap^t Anno Dom. 1724. [B fol. 9 v.

Mary the Daughter of Thomas Beckwith of Coniston Lab. Bap^t July the 19th
William the Son of Anthony Allan of Coniston Lab. Bap^t July the 26th
Jane the Daughter of Joseph Hesletine of Kilnsey Miner Bap^t August the 30th
Doratha the Daughter of Joseph Horner of Coniston Lab. Bap^t September the 14th
Elizabeth the Daughter of Henry Ovington of Kilnsey Lab. Bap^t December the 13th
Grace the Daughter of John Preston of Kilnsey Black Smith Bap^t February the 3^d
John the Son of Henry Constantine of Coniston Yeom' Bap^t Febuary the 28th
Henry the Son of Henry Constantine of Coniston Yeom' Bap^t March the 1st
Elizabeth the Daughter of Robert Stoyles of Kilnsey Lab. Bap^t March the 1st

Nom: Nup: Anno Dom. 1725.

William Horsforth of Hetton Linen Weaver & Ann Downham of Coniston Spinster married January the Second by M^r Jn^o Anderton bands thrice published by the parsons of Burnsall.

Nom: Bap^t Anno Dom: 1725.

Roger the Son of Thomas Bolton of Kilnsey Yeom' Bap^t May the 12th

Sarah the Daughter of John Waterhouse of Kilnsey Miner Bap[t] June the 6[th]

Anna the Daughter of Jn[o] Constantine of Coniston Yeom' Bap[t] June the 13[th]

Mary the Daughter of Danell Preston of Kilnsey Cordwainer Bap[t] June the 25.

Mary the Daughter of Jn[o] Tattersall of Coniston Inkeeper Bap[t] August the 1[st]

Mary the Daughter of Robert Ellis of Coniston Lab : Bap[t] October the 24[th]

Robert the Son of Jn[o] Tennant of Chappelhouse Gen[t] Bap[t] January the 14.

Edward the Son of Edward Hesletine of Kilnsey Miner Bap[t] Febuary the 13[th]

Burialls none 1725.

---

[In the margin is written "Lawrence Holiday Mary," and at the bottom of the page "Henry Ovington Kilnsay 1785." Ed.]

[C fol. 1 r.

A true Register of all Marriages Christings and Burialls that have been at the parachall Chapp' of Coniston within the p$^{r}$ish of Burnsall since the begining of the Year of o$^{r}$ Lord God 1726.

Nom. Bap$^{t}$ Anno Dom. 1726.

John the Son of John Winder of Kilnsey Lab. Bap$^{t}$ Apprill the 17$^{th}$
James the Son of Laurence Holiday of Kilnsey Yeom' Bap$^{t}$ May the 29$^{th}$
Anne the Daught$^{r}$ of Henry Ovington of Kilnsey Yeom' Bap$^{t}$ Aug$^{t}$ the 21$^{th}$
Joseph the Son of Joseph Hesletine of Kilnsey Miner Bap$^{t}$ Novemb$^{r}$ the 2$^{d}$
Joseph the Son of Jos : Horner of Coniston Lab : Bap$^{t}$ Octob$^{r}$ the 16$^{th}$
Alice the Daught$^{r}$ of Henry Constantine of Coniston Yeom' Bap$^{t}$ Novemb$^{r}$ the 27$^{th}$
Anne the Daught$^{r}$ of Rob$^{t}$ Stoyles of Kilnsey Lab : Bap$^{t}$ March the 5$^{th}$
Thomas the Son of Jon$^{o}$ Constantine of Coniston Yeom' Bap$^{t}$ March the 12$^{th}$

Nom : Sepull$^{t}$ Anno Dom. 1726.

William Sidgesweek of Kilnsey Pentioner buried Apprill the 9$^{th}$
Esther the Daught$^{r}$ of Edward Hesletine of Kilnsey Miner buried June the 21$^{st}$
James the Son of Lau : Holiday of Kilnsey Yeom' buried Aug$^{t}$ the 18$^{th}$
Alice the Daught$^{r}$ of Hen : Constantine of Coniston Yom' buried October the 4$^{th}$
Dorratha the Wife of Tho$^{s}$ Beckwith of Coniston Lab. buried Decemb$^{r}$ the 26.

Marriages none 1726.

Nom : Bap$^{t}$ Anno Dom : 1727.

Thomas the Son of Low : Wildeman of Coniston Lab : bap$^{t}$ Apprill y$^{e}$ 2$^{d}$
Sarah y$^{e}$ Daug : of James Robinson of Kilnsey Lab : bap$^{t}$ Apprill y$^{e}$ 9$^{th}$
Thomas y$^{e}$ Son of Henry Constantine of Coniston Yeom' bap$^{t}$ May y$^{e}$ 14$^{th}$
Izatt y$^{e}$ Daug : of Felix Preston of Kilnsey Blacksmith bap$^{t}$ June y$^{e}$ 11$^{th}$
Margrett y$^{e}$ Daug : of Lowrance Holiday of Kilnsey Yeom' bap$^{t}$ August y$^{e}$ 27$^{th}$
Elizabeth y$^{e}$ Daug : of John Constantine of Coniston Yeom' bap$^{t}$ Decemb$^{r}$ y$^{e}$ 10$^{th}$
Thomas y$^{e}$ Son of John Winder of Kilnsey Lab : bap$^{t}$ Feb : y$^{e}$ 11$^{th}$
John y$^{e}$ Son of Thomas Bolton of Kilnsey Yeom' bap$^{t}$ March y$^{e}$ 10$^{th}$

Nom. Sepul$^{t}$ Anno Dom. 1727.

Mary y$^{e}$ Wife of Robert Ibbotson of Coniston Lab. buried June y$^{e}$ 28$^{th}$
Fran : Daug : of John Constantine of Coniston Yeom' buried January y$^{e}$ 18$^{th}$
Margrett y$^{e}$ Wife of Jonathan Constantine of Coniston Yeom' buried January y$^{e}$ 31$^{st}$

Marriages none 1727.

Nom. Bap$^{t}$ Anno Dom. 1728.

John the Son of Henry Ovington of Kilnsey Lab. Bap$^{t}$ March y$^{e}$ 30$^{th}$
Edward the Son of John Tennant of Chapp'house Gen$^{t}$ Bap$^{t}$ May the 2$^{d}$
William the Son of Francis Duckett of Kilnsey Lab. Bap$^{t}$ August the 20$^{th}$
John the Son of John Ellis of Coniston Carpinter Bap$^{t}$ August the 25$^{th}$
Jonathan the Son of Henry Constantine of Coniston Husbandman Bap$^{t}$ September y$^{e}$ 30$^{th}$
Sarah the Daughter of Mary Lawson being a bastard Child Bap$^{t}$ October y$^{e}$ 20$^{th}$
Mary the Daughter of Joseph Hesletine of Kilnsey Miner Bap$^{t}$ Feb: y$^{e}$ 5$^{th}$

Nom. Sepult. Anno Dom. 1728.

John the Son of Henry Ovington of Kilnsey Lab. buried Aprill y$^{e}$ 3$^{th}$
Agnes the Wife of Henry Ovington afores$^{d}$ buried August y$^{e}$ 4$^{th}$
Frances Constantine Widd. & relict of John Constantine of Coniston dsd. buried Octob$^{r}$ the first.
Thomas the Son of Henry Constantine of Coniston Yeom' buried Novemb$^{r}$ the 16$^{th}$
Thomas the Son of John Winder of Kilnsey Lab: buried Novemb$^{r}$ the 22$^{d}$
Jonathan the Son of Henry Constantine of Coniston Husbandman buried Feb: y$^{e}$ 1$^{st}$
Frances Constantine Widdow & relict of Jonathan Constantine of Coniston dec$^{d}$ buried Feb. y$^{e}$ 4$^{th}$
Elizabeth y$^{e}$ Daughter of George Horner of Coniston dec$^{d}$ buried Feb: y$^{e}$ 20$^{th}$

Marriages none 1728.

Nom. Bap$^{t}$ Anno Dom. 1729. [C fol. 1 v.

John the Son of Richard Constantine of Coniston Yeom' Bap$^{t}$ May the 3$^{d}$
Margrett the Daughter of Henry Constantine of Coniston Yeom' Bap$^{t}$ June the 10$^{th}$
Mary the Daughter of Robert Stoyles of Coniston Lab. Bap$^{t}$ July the 20$^{th}$
Jonathan the Son of Henry Constantine of Coniston Husbandman dec$^{d}$ Bap$^{t}$ Septemb$^{r}$ y$^{e}$ 28$^{th}$
Mary the Daughter of John Winder of Kilnsey Lab. Bap$^{t}$ November the 30$^{th}$
Margrett the Daug$^{t}$ of Thomas Ibbotson of Coniston Lab. Bap$^{t}$ Febuary the 10$^{th}$
Elizabeth the Daug$^{t}$ of Lowrance Holiday Yeom' Bap$^{t}$ March the 5$^{th}$
Richard the Son of John Tennant of Chapp'house Gen$^{t}$ Bap$^{t}$ March the 18$^{th}$

Nom: Nup$^{t}$ Anno Dom. 1729.

Thomas Ibbotson of Coniston Lab. & Ann Mallison of the same Spinster married by M$^{r}$ Pot$^{t}$ Alcock 14$^{th}$ of July bands thrice published by the Parsons of Burnsall.

Edmund Robinson of Northcoat Labo^r^ & Mary Preston of Kilnsey Spinster married by M^r^ Pet^r^ Alcock Febuary y^e^ 10^th^ bands thrice published by the Parsons of Burnsall.

Henry Ibbotson of Linton Lab. & Agnes Mallison of Coniston Spinster married by M^r^ Pet^r^ Alcock Febuary y^e^ 10^th^ bands thrice published by the Parsons of Burnsall & Certified by M^r^ James Roberts Rec^t^ of Linton.

Nom : Sepull^t^ Anno Dom. 1729.

Mary the Daug : of Joseph Hesletine of Kilnsey Miner buried Aprill y^e^ 21^st^

John the Son of Richard Constantine of Coniston Yeom' buried May y^e^ 10^th^

Henry Constantine of Coniston Husbandman buried May y^e^ 20^th^

Jane Constantine of Coniston Spinster buried June y^e^ 8^th^

John Winsor of Coniston paup^r^ buried June y^e^ 11^th^

Thomas Johnson of Kilnsey paup^r^ buried June y^e^ 15^th^

Thomas the Son of John Tattersall of Coniston Inkeep^r^ buried July y^e^ 21^st^

Issabell the Wife of Thomas Bradley of Kilnsey Millner buried March y^e^ 18^th^

Nom. Bap^t^ Anno Dom. 1730.

Ann the Daug^t^ of James Robinson of Kilnsey Lab^r^ Bap^t^ June y^e^ 7^th^

Humphrey the Son of Rich : Constantine of Coniston Yeom' Bap^t^ July y^e^ 12^th^

John the Son of Robert Holdgate of Kilnsey Yeom' Bap^t^ October y^e^ 25^th^

Hellen the Daug^t^ of John Abbotson of Northcoat Yeom' Bap^t^ November y^e^ 1^st^

Rebecca the Daug^t^ of William Duckett of Kilnsey Lab^r^ Bap^t^ March y^e^ 16^th^

Nom. Sepull^t^ Anno Dom. 1730.

Elizabeth Johnson of Kilnsey Spinst^r^ buried Aprill y^e^ 7^th^

Robert the Son of James Ibbotson Cordwainer buried May y^e^ 14^th^

Humphrey the Son of Rich^d^ Constantine of Coniston Yeom' buried August y^e^ 13^th^

Henry Ibbotson of Kilnsey Yeom' buried December y^e^ 21^st^

Nom : Bap^t^ Anno Dom. 1731.

Barbara the Daug^t^ of Jn^o^ Ellis of Coniston Carpint^r^ Bap^t^ May y^e^ 2^d^

Agnes the Daug^t^ of Joseph Hesletine of Kilnsey Miner Bap^t^ July y^e^ 20^th^

Rachel the Daug^t^ of Edward Hesletine of Kilnsey Miner Bap^t^ October ye 10^th^

Robert the Son of Thomas Ibbotson of Coniston Lab^r^ Bap^t^ October y^e^ 10^th^

William the Son of Jn^o^ Parker of Coniston Lab^r^ Bap^t^ December y^e^ 5^th^

Giles the Son of Jn^o^ Tennant of Chapp'house Gen^t^ Bap^t^ December y^e^ 17^th^

Hellen the Daug^t^ of Henry Constantine of Coniston Yeom' Bap^t^ January y^e^ 17^th^

Elizabeth the Daug$^{t}$ of Jn$^{o}$ Winder of Kilnsey Lab$^{r}$ Bap$^{t}$ Febuary y$^{e}$ 27$^{th}$

Samuel the Son of Richard Constantine of Coniston Yeom' Bap$^{t}$ March y$^{e}$ 19$^{th}$

Jonathan the Son of Richard Constantine of Coniston Yeom' Bap$^{t}$ March y$^{e}$ 19$^{th}$

Nom. Sepull$^{t}$ Anno Dom. 1731.

Rebecca the Daug$^{t}$ of William Duckett of Kilnsey Lab$^{r}$ buried May y$^{e}$ 22$^{d}$

James Sidgeswick of Kilnsey paup$^{r}$ buried May y$^{e}$ 27$^{th}$

William Horner of Coniston Taylor buried December y$^{e}$ 26$^{th}$

Mary Wife of Thomas Pulman of Coniston Innkeep$^{r}$ buried March y$^{e}$ 4$^{th}$

Marriages none Anno Dom. 1731.

Nom. Nup$^{t}$ Anno Dom. 1732.

Edward Hesletine of Kilnsey Miner and Alice Duffeild of Kilnsey Spinster was married February y$^{e}$ 5$^{th}$ by M$^{r}$ John Alcock by vertue of a Licence signed by Roger Mitton Surg$^{t}$

[C fol. 2 r.

The Names of those Baptized in the Year of our Lord 1736.

John the Son of John Serjeantson of Coniston Miner bap$^{t}$ April the 4$^{th}$

Elizabeth the Daughter of Robert Hallam of Kilnsey Miner bap$^{t}$ October the 24$^{th}$

The Names of those Buried in the Year of our Lord 1736.

Hellen the Daughter of Thomas Hebden of Coniston Yeom' Buried June the 19$^{th}$

Jane Holmes of Kilnsey Widd. Buried January the 1$^{st}$

The Names of those Married in the Year of our Lord 1736.

John Blakebrough Weaver and Frances Constantine Spinster both of the Parish of Bingley Bands published & Certified by M$^{r}$ T. Ferrand Vic: of Bingley Married by M$^{r}$ Will: Tompson Curate at Burnsall Febuary the 13$^{th}$

The Names of those Baptized in the Year of our Lord 1737.

Ellen the Daughter of Henry Ovington of Kilnsey Yeom' Baptized June the 12$^{th}$

Elianor the Daughter of Henry Ellis of Coniston Joyner Baptized October the 27$^{th}$

Christian the Daughter of John Winder of Kilnsey Myner Baptized January the first.

The Names of those Buried in the Year of our Lord 1737.

John Constantine of Coniston Yeom' Buried May the 14$^{th}$

Margrett the Daughter of Henry Constantine of Coniston Yeom' Buried November the 30$^{th}$

The Names of those Married in the Year 1737.

Luke Horner Glover and Martha Jackson Spinster both of Coniston bands thrice published by the parsons of Burnsall Married by M$^{r}$ Mat: Knowles Curate at Burnsall October the 3$^{d}$

The Names of those Baptized in the Year of our Lord 1738.

Richard the Son of John Blakebrooke Searge weaver Baptized Aprill y^e^ 2^d^
Mary the Daughter of Joseph Waddilove of Coniston Yeom' Baptized May the 15^th^
William the Son of Robert Stoyles of Coniston Miner Baptized June the 11^th^
John the Son of Thomas Holdgate of Coniston Farmer Baptized June the 24^th^
George the Son of Luke Horner of Coniston Glover Baptized June the 25^th^
Robert the Son of Robert Hallam of Kilusey Miner Baptized June the 25^th^
Barbara the Daughter of William Beecroft of Coniston Labourer Baptized July the 25^th^
Issabell the Daughter of John Tomlinson of Kilnsey Milner Baptized November the 12^th^
John the Son of Francis Duckitt of Kilnsey Farmer Baptized March the 25^th^

The Names of those Buried in the Year of our Lord 1738.

Mary Preston a Poor Woman Buried May the 9^th^
Daniell Preston of Kilnsey Labourer Buried July the 15^th^
Thomas Waterhouse Miner Buried December the 30^th^

Marriages none 1738.

The Names of those Baptized in the Year of o^r^ Lord 1739.

John the Son of Francis Duckett of Kilnsey Labourer Baptized March the 25^th^
Issabell the Daughter of Henry Ellis of Kilnsey Carpenter Baptized June the 17^th^
Richard the Son of Thomas Duckett of Kilnsey Myner Baptized October the 28^th^
Tomasin the Daughter of Henry Layland of Coniston Yeom' Baptized March the 23^d^

The Names of those Buried in the Year of o^r^ Lord 1739.

John Ellis of Coniston Carpenter Buried February the 9^th^

Marriages none 1739.

Nom: Bap^t^ Anno Dom. 1732. [C fol. 2 v.

Ann the Daug^t^ of Francis Duckett of Kilnsey Lab^r^ Bap^t^ Aprill the 16^th^
Jane the Daug^t^ of Robert Stoyles of Coniston Lab^r^ Bap^t^ May y^e^ 3^d^
Henry the Son of Henry Ovington of Kilnsey Yeom' Bap^t^ June y^e^ 20^th^
Thomasin Daug^t^ of Martha Rathmill of Kilnsey being a Bastard Child Bap^t^ October y^e^ 2^d^
Hellen the Daug^t^ of Lowrance Holiday of Kilnsey Yeom' Bap^t^ December y^e^ 3^d^
John the Son of James Robinson of Kilnsey Lab^r^ Bap^t^ December y^e^ 24^th^

Nom: Sepull^t Anno Dom 1732.

Samuell the Son of Richard Constantine Yeom^r buried March y^e 27^th
Elizabeth Thistlewhite of Kilnsey Widd. buried Aprill the 14^th
Isabell the Wife of John Abbotson of Northcoat Yeom^r buried May the 3^d
Jane the Wife of Edward Hesletine of Kilnsey Miner buried May the 17^th
Robert the Son of Thomas Pulman of Coniston Lab^r buried July the 27^th
Hellen the Daugh^t of John Parker of Coniston Lab^r buried December the 4^th
Barbra the Daug^t of John Ellis of Coniston Carpint^r buried February the 6^th
William the Son of John Parker of Coniston Lab^r buried February the 24^th
Jonathan the Son of Richard Constantine of Coniston Yeom^r buried February the 26^th
Martha the Daug^t of Henry Constantine of Skipton Mercer buried March the 1^st

The Names of those Baptized in the Year of our Lord 1733.

Mary the Daug^t of Robert Holdgate of Kilnsey Yeom^r Bap^t Aprill the 8^th
[Alice the Daug^t of Thomas Duckett of Kilnsey Lab^r Bap^t July the first.]
John the Son of William Duckett of Kilnsey Lab^r Bap^t July the 2^d
Alice the Daug^t of John Tennant of Chapp'house Gen^t Bap^t August the 6^th
Frances the Daug^t of John Constantine of Coniston Yeom^r Bap^t December the 23^d

The Names of those Buried in the Year of our Lord 1733.

William the Son of Henry Simpson of Coniston Yeom^r Buried May the 7^th
Alice the Daug^t of John Tennant of Chapp'house Gen^t buried August the 26^th
Mary the Daug^t of Robert Holdgate of Kilnsey Yeom^r buried September the 26^th
Charles Abbotson of Coniston Yeom^r Buried February the 4^th

Mariages None in the Year of our Lord 1733.

The Names of those Baptized in the Year of our Lord 1734.

John the Son of William Beecroft of Coniston Lab^r Bap^t June the 16^th
Richard the Son of Robert Holdgate of Kilnsey Yeom^r Bap^t July the 21^st
William the Son of Robert Hallam of Kilnsey Miner Bap^t July the 28^th
Joseph the Son of John Ellis of Coniston Joyner Bap^t October the 13^th
Tomasin the Daughter of John Tennant of Chapp'house Gen^t Bap^t November the 27^th
Hellen the Daughter of Thomas Hebden of Coniston Yeom^r Bap^t January the 31^st

Francis the Son of Henry Ovington of Kilnsey Yeom' Bap$^{t}$ Febuary the 2$^{d}$
Agnes the Daughter of John Winder of Kilnsey Miner Bap$^{t}$ Febuary the 16$^{th}$
Mary the Daughter of Thomas Duckitt of Kilnsey Miner Bap$^{t}$ March the 2$^{d}$

The Names of those Buried in the Year of our Lord 1734.

Dorratha the Daughter of Lowrance Wildeman of Coniston Lab$^{r}$ buried Aprill the 2$^{d}$
Rebecca the Wife of Thomas Wigglesworth of Coniston Yeom' buried October the 10$^{th}$
William the Son of Anthony Allan of Coniston Lab$^{r}$ buried March the 7$^{th}$

Marriages None in the Year of our Lord 1734.

The Names of those Bapized in the Year of our Lord 1735.

Rebecca the Daughter of Francis Duckett of Kilnsey Labourer Bap$^{t}$ Aprill the 22.
John the Son of Joseph Hesletine of Kilnsey Miner Bap$^{t}$ May the 10$^{th}$
John the Son of Robert Stoyles of Coniston Lab$^{r}$ Bap$^{t}$ May the 21$^{st}$
William the Son of Thomas Ibbotson of Coniston Lab$^{r}$ Bap$^{t}$ August the 10$^{th}$
Robert the Son of James Paley of Kilnsey Lab$^{r}$ Bap$^{t}$ November the 9$^{th}$
Ann the Daughter of William Beecroft of Coniston Lab$^{r}$ Bap$^{t}$ Febuary the 8.

The Names of those buried in the Year of our Lord 1735.

Elizabeth the Wife of Daniell Preston of Kilnsey Miner buried January the 31$^{st}$

Marriages none in the Year of our Lord 1735.

[C fol. 3 r.

*The Names of those Married at Coniston Chapp$^{ll}$ in the Year 1740.

............of the p$^{r}$ish of Arncliffe and Ann Hallam of Coniston .........
............Aprill the 19$^{th}$ 1740 by M$^{r}$ William Thompson Curate.........
............published in the p$^{r}$ish Churches of Arncliffe ....................
............Farmer and Sarah Slinger of Chappell ..........................
............the 30$^{th}$ 1740 by M$^{r}$ John Alcock Rect$^{r}$...........

............zed in the Year 1740.

............roft of Coniston Lab$^{r}$ Baptized November the 2$^{d}$ 1740.
............der of Kilnsey Myner Baptized December the 14$^{th}$
............lis of Kilnsey Carpinter Baptized January the 25$^{th}$ 1740.
... ........of Coniston Glover Baptized Febuary the 8$^{th}$ 1740.

...........Buried in the Year 1740.

...........lgate buried November the 6$^{th}$ 1740.
... ........sey Spinster buried November the 21$^{st}$ 1740.
John Serjeantson of Coniston a Poor man buried December the 18$^{th}$ 1740.

* A corner of the leaf has been torn off.

The Names of those Married at Coniston Chappell in y$^{e}$ year 1741.

M$^{r}$ Josias Dawson of Haltongill in y$^{e}$ Parish of Arncliff and M$^{s}$ Susannah Constantine of Coniston was Married att Conisstone Chappell August y$^{e}$ 27$^{th}$ 1741 by M$^{r}$ William Tompson Curatt by Vertue of a Lisance.

John Stackhouse of Burnsal Carpinter and Elizabeth Horner of Conistone spinster was Married September y$^{e}$ 28$^{th}$ 1741 by M$^{r}$ Matthew Knowls Curat thrice published in y$^{e}$ Parris Church.

The Names of those Baptized in y$^{e}$ Year 1741.

Robert y$^{e}$ Son of Robert Hallam Miner was Baptized y$^{e}$ 3$^{d}$ Day of May.

Robert y$^{e}$ Son of Robert Stoyles Miner was Baptized y$^{e}$ 3$^{d}$ Day of August.

The Names of those Buried in y$^{e}$ year 1741.

Lawrance Wildman was Buried y$^{e}$ 26$^{th}$ Day ol March.
William Slinger was Buried y$^{e}$ 31$^{st}$ Day of March.
Richard Ellis was Buried y$^{e}$ 5$^{th}$ Day of June.
Thomas Wigglesworth was Buried y$^{e}$ 27$^{th}$ Day of August.
Margret y$^{e}$ Wife of John Tatterson was Buried y$^{e}$ 12$^{th}$ Day of September.

The Names of those Baptized in y$^{e}$ Year 1742.

Agnes the Daughter of thomas tomlinson laberer Baptized July y$^{e}$ 2 day.

The Names of those Bvryed In y$^{e}$ year 1742.

Henry Ovington of Kilnsey Yeom' was Bvryed y$^{e}$ 26$^{th}$ day of october.

Mariges none In y$^{e}$ year 1742.

Names of Those Married at Conistone Chappell in y$^{e}$ year 1743.

John Clark of Northcoat and Ann Constantine Marrid May the 10$^{d}$ 1743 by Bands with the Reverend Matthew Knowles.

1744 Baptisms. [C fol. 3 v.

Isabel the Daugh$^{r}$ of Tho$^{s}$ Thomlinson Labourer Baptized May the 27$^{th}$
Ann Windra the Daughter of John Windra Minor Bap$^{d}$ June y$^{e}$ 17.
Ann Bawdwin the Daugh$^{r}$ of William Bawdwin Labourer Bapt$^{d}$ July y$^{e}$ 22$^{d}$

1745 Baptisms.

Elisabeth the Daugh$^{r}$ of W$^{m}$ Clark Minor Bapti$^{d}$ Aug$^{t}$ y$^{e}$ 25$^{th}$
Agnes the Daugh$^{r}$ of Hen$^{ry}$ Hebdin Minor Bapt$^{d}$ N$^{r}$ y$^{e}$ 15$^{th}$
W$^{m}$ the Son of W$^{m}$ Beecroft Minor Bapt$^{d}$ March y$^{e}$ 2$^{d}$

Burials.

Josua the Son of Henry Hebdin Minor Buried June y$^{e}$ 20$^{th}$
Tho$^{s}$ the Son of Jonathan Constantine Yeaman Buried Sept$^{r}$ y$^{e}$ 28$^{th}$
Mary Wildman Spinster Buried Oct$^{r}$ y$^{e}$ 14$^{th}$
Marg$^{t}$ Horner Widdow Buried March y$^{e}$ 23$^{d}$

1746.

1747 Baptizms. [C fol. 4 r.

Rob$^{t}$ y$^{e}$ Son of John Windra Bapti$^{d}$ May y$^{e}$ 10$^{th}$
John y$^{e}$ Son of Chrs$^{r}$ Petty Inkeeper Bapti$^{d}$ Aug$^{t}$ y$^{e}$ 2$^{d}$
Ann the Daug$^{t}$ of Tho$^{s}$ Ibbotson Labourer Bapti$^{d}$ March y$^{e}$ 13$^{th}$

### Burials.

Elizabeth Windra Poor Woman Buried March y$^{e}$ 30$^{th}$
Ann y$^{e}$ Wife of Rob$^{t}$ Stoyls Buried July y$^{e}$ 12$^{th}$

### 1748 Marriages.

Joseph Pearson of Kettlewell Taylor and Mary Bradley of Kilnsay Spinster married by M$^{r}$ Knowles by Banns Dec$^{r}$ y$^{e}$ 3$^{d}$

### Baptisms.

George the Son of W$^{m}$ Beecroft Labourer Bapt$^{d}$ May the 7$^{th}$
Tho$^{s}$ the Son of John Needham Minor Bapt$^{d}$ July y$^{e}$ 10$^{th}$
John the Son of Henry Ellis Joyner Bapt$^{d}$ July y$^{e}$ 23$^{d}$
Ann the Daughter of Rich$^{d}$ Duckitt Bapt$^{d}$ Dec$^{r}$ y$^{e}$ 18$^{th}$
James the Son of Tho$^{s}$ Thomlinson Bapt$^{d}$ Aug$^{t}$ y$^{e}$ 6$^{th}$
Elisebeth y$^{e}$ Daug$^{r}$ of John Whitaker Farmer Bap$^{d}$ Aug$^{t}$ y$^{e}$ 10$^{th}$
Isabel the Daugh$^{r}$ of Henry Whitam Coardwainer Bapti$^{d}$ y$^{e}$ 5$^{th}$ March.
Dina the Daugh$^{r}$ of Rob$^{t}$ Stoney Mason Bapt$^{d}$ March y$^{e}$ 5$^{th}$
John the Son of W$^{m}$ Bawdwin Labourer Bapt$^{d}$ March y$^{e}$ 19$^{th}$

### Burials.

Edward ye Son of W$^{m}$ Bawdwin Labourer Buried Aug$^{t}$ y$^{e}$ 8$^{th}$
Jane y$^{e}$ Wife of W$^{m}$ Beecroft Labourer Buried Sep$^{r}$ y$^{e}$ 27$^{th}$
Jane y$^{e}$ Wife of John Middlebrook Buried N$^{r}$ y$^{e}$ 9$^{th}$

### 1749 Marriages.

Tho$^{s}$ Rypley Miner in Grassington in y$^{e}$ Parish of Linton and Elizabeth Jennam Spinster in Conniston in y$^{e}$ Parish of Burnsall and Married by M$^{r}$ Matthew Knowles on y$^{e}$ 26$^{th}$ Day of January.

### Baptisms.

Elisabeth the Daughter of Rich$^{d}$ Bolland Farmer in Conniston Bapt$^{d}$ Dec$^{r}$ y$^{e}$ 3$^{d}$ by y$^{e}$ Rev$^{d}$ M$^{r}$ John Alcock.
Margaret y$^{e}$ Daugh$^{r}$ of Mary Beckwith a Bastard Child Bapt$^{d}$ Ja$^{r}$ y$^{e}$ 21$^{st}$

### Burials.

Ellin Clark Spinster Buried Sep$^{r}$ y$^{e}$ 2$^{d}$
Alce the Doughter of Rob$^{t}$ Hallam Miner Babz$^{d}$ Sep$^{r}$ 17$^{th}$ 1768.
W$^{m}$ the Son of Rob$^{t}$ Hallam Miner Babz$^{d}$ Aug$^{t}$ 27 1770 By the Rev$^{d}$ John Alcock.
Dolley the Doughter of W$^{m}$ Hallam Miner Babtiz$^{d}$ Jan$^{y}$ 10$^{d}$ 1773 By the Rev$^{d}$ John Alcock.
Isabel the Doughter of John Mason Labourer Babtiz$^{d}$ Jan$^{y}$ 17$^{d}$ 1773 By the Rev$^{d}$ John Alcock.
Thomas the Son of Richard Blackay Labouor Babtiz$^{d}$ Jan$^{y}$ the 31$^{st}$ 1773 By the Rever$^{d}$ John Alcock.

### 1750 Marriages. [C fol. 4 v.

Anthony Hepper and Suanna Ibbotson was married by M$^{r}$ John Hewit Aprill 24$^{th}$
James Nelson and Mary Stoyles was married N$^{r}$ y$^{e}$ 2$^{d}$

Baptisms.

James y$^{e}$ Son of James Middlebrook Bapt$^{d}$ Oct$^{r}$ y$^{e}$ 21$^{st}$
Henry y$^{e}$ Son of Henry Ellis Bapt$^{d}$ N$^{r}$ y$^{e}$ 3$^{d}$
Ann y$^{e}$ Daugh$^{r}$ of Rob$^{r}$ Lucas Bapt$^{d}$ N$^{r}$ y$^{e}$ 25$^{th}$
Jane y$^{e}$ Daugh$^{r}$ of Henry Layland Bapt$^{d}$ Feb$^{ry}$ y$^{e}$ 21$^{th}$
Rich$^{d}$ the Son of Rich$^{d}$ Duckitt Bapt$^{d}$ Janu$^{ry}$ y$^{e}$ 27$^{th}$
Alice y$^{e}$ Daugh$^{r}$ of Rich$^{d}$ Duckitt Bapt$^{d}$ January y$^{e}$ 27$^{th}$

Burials.

Roger Preston Buried N$^{r}$ y$^{e}$ 11$^{th}$

1751 Marriages.

W$^{m}$ Clark Servant Man and Margaret Ibbotson Spinster was married att Conniston Chapell May y$^{e}$ 26$^{th}$

Baptisms.

Elizabeth the Daugh$^{r}$ of W$^{m}$ Bawdin Labouer Bap$^{d}$ April y$^{e}$ 7$^{th}$
Laurans y$^{e}$ Son of Tho$^{s}$ Thomlinson Labourer Bap$^{d}$ May y$^{e}$ 7$^{th}$
Rob$^{t}$ y$^{e}$ Son of Mary Dickisson being a Bastard Child was Bapti$^{d}$ Dec$^{r}$ y$^{e}$ 24$^{th}$
John y$^{e}$ Son of W$^{m}$ Clark Labourer Baptized March y$^{e}$ 15$^{th}$
Ann y$^{e}$ Daugh$^{r}$ of W$^{m}$ Hawworth Labourer Bapt$^{d}$ March y$^{e}$ 18$^{th}$

Burials.

Elisabeth y$^{e}$ Daugh$^{r}$ of W$^{m}$ Bawdin Buried Aug$^{st}$ y$^{e}$ 11$^{th}$
W$^{m}$ y$^{e}$ Son of W$^{m}$ Beecroft Labourer Buried Dec$^{r}$ y$^{e}$ 15$^{th}$
Jane y$^{e}$ Daugh$^{r}$ of Henry Layland Yeaman Buried Dec$^{r}$ y$^{e}$ 21$^{st}$
Thomasin y$^{e}$ Daugh$^{r}$ of Henry Layland Yeaman Buried Dec$^{r}$ y$^{e}$ 25$^{th}$
John y$^{e}$ Son of John Whitaker Farmer Buried Janu$^{ry}$ y$^{e}$ 8$^{th}$
Henry y$^{e}$ Son of Henry Ellis Joyner Buried Jan$^{ry}$ y$^{e}$ 11$^{th}$
Rob$^{t}$ Nelson Buried Janu$^{ry}$ 29$^{th}$
Ellin y$^{e}$ Daughter of Mary Tatterson be a Bastard Buried Janu$^{ry}$ 30$^{th}$

Marriages 1752.

Tho$^{s}$ Joy Labourer and Agnes Parker Spinster Married April y$^{e}$ 1$^{st}$ by Banns.
W$^{m}$ Slinger Yeaman and Mary Knowles Spinster Married May y$^{e}$ 20$^{th}$ by Banns.
W$^{m}$ Beecroft Labourer and Mary Tennant Spinster Married May y$^{e}$ 21$^{st}$ by Banns.

Baptisms.

Marg$^{t}$ y$^{e}$ Daugh$^{r}$ of John Petty Labourer Bapti$^{d}$ July y$^{e}$ 12$^{th}$
Stephen y$^{e}$ Son of Lupton Wrathall Yeaman Baptised July y$^{e}$ 12$^{th}$
Tho$^{s}$ ye Son of Mary Beckwith a Bastard Child Baptized July y$^{e}$ 26$^{th}$
Mary y$^{e}$ Daughter of John Mallison Taylor Bapti$^{d}$ Aug$^{t}$ y$^{e}$ 16$^{th}$
Edward y$^{e}$ Son of Jane Stoyles a Bastard Child Baptised Sep$^{r}$ y$^{e}$ 24$^{th}$
Hanna y$^{e}$ Daughter of James Middlebrook Joyner Baptised Oct$^{r}$ y$^{e}$ 26$^{th}$
Mary y$^{e}$ Daughter of Henry Ellis Joyner Baptised N$^{r}$ y$^{e}$ 26$^{th}$
Jane y$^{e}$ Daughter of John Whitaker Farmer Baptised Dec$^{r}$ y$^{e}$ 31$^{th}$
Hanna y$^{e}$ Daughter of Henry Layland Yeaman Baptised Dec$^{r}$ y$^{e}$ 21$^{th}$
Jane y$^{e}$ Daughter of W$^{m}$ Bawdin Labourer Baptised January y$^{e}$ 14$^{th}$
Isabel y$^{e}$ Daughter of W$^{m}$ Beecrof Baptised February y$^{e}$ 25$^{th}$
Marg$^{t}$ y$^{e}$ Daughter of W$^{m}$ Slinger Yeaman Baptised March y$^{e}$ 4$^{th}$

Burials.

James Tennant Yeaman Buried Fabuary ye 16th
Laurance Holyday Yeaman Buried March ye 9th
Isabel ye Daughter of Wm Beecroft Labourer Buried March ye 13th
Fælix Priston Blacksmith Buried March ye 18th

1753 Marriages. [C fol. 5 r.

Stephen Falshaw Servant Man and Jane Stead Married by Banns April ye 27th
Thos Lupton and Dorethy Horner Spinster Married June ye 18th
James Sawer Miner Isat Preston Spinster Married Octor ye 4th
Robt Holgate Farmer and Ellin Holgate Spinster Married Decr 27th Banns.
John Robinson Farmer and Ann Latham Spinster Married Febry 7th Banns.

Baptisms.

Agnes ye Daughter of Collumbus Ingleby Gentleman Baptised April ye 1st
Elisabeth ye Daughter of Richd Duckitt Horse Breaker Baptised July ye 8th
Barbara ye Daughter of John Needham Baptised Sepr ye 10th

Burials.

Marmaduke ye Son of John Needham Miner Buried Augst ye 29th
Francis ye Son of John Needham Miner Buried Sepr ye 7th
Margat Slinger Buried February ye 11th
Francis Needham Buried March ye 14th

1754 Baptisms.

Joseph ye Son of Thos Lupton Miner Baptisd May ye 19th
John ye Son of John Petty Husbandman Bapd May ye 21st
Fælix ye Son of James Sawer Miner Baptsd Augt ye 11th
Mary ye Daughtr of Wm Beecroft Labourer Bapd Augt ye 18th
Elisabeth ye Daugr of Wm Hawwith Labourer Bapd Nr ye 24th
Thos ye Son of Thos Ibbotson Labourer Baptid Janry 26th
Susanna ye Daughr of Lupton Wrathall Farmer Baptd Fabvary 23d
Ann ye Daughr of Henry Ellis Joyner Bapd Fabvary 23d

Burials.

Ellin ye Daughr Laurance Holyday Buried Sepr ye 17th

1755 Baptisms.

Wm ye Son of Wm Slinger Yeaman Baptd June ye 1st
Alexandria ye Son of Alexandria Macbain Soldier Bapd June ye 8th
Wm ye Son of James Middlebrook Joyner Bapd Sepr ye 28th
Thos ye Son of Wm Clark Labourer Baptd Nr ye 2d
Matthew ye Son of James Sawer Miner Baptid Fabury ye 2d
John ye Son of Henry Layland Yeaman Baptsd March ye 16th

Burials.

Barbara ye Daugr of John Needham Miner Burd May ye 4th
Robt ye Son of Thos Ibbotson Labourer Buried May ye 15th

Mary ye Wife of Robr Mallison Taylor Buried July ye 7th
John Needham Miner Buried Augt ye 22d
Isat the Wife of James Sawer Miner Buried Febuary ye 2d

1756 Baptisms.

James ye Son of Thos Thomlinson Labourer Bapd April ye 20th
Mary ye Daughr of Wm Bawdin Bapd ye 6th of June.
Alice ye Daughr of Robr Slinger Yeaman Bapd July ye 9th
Francis ye Son of Thos Petty Husbandman Baptid Augst ye 20th
Wm ye Son of Wm Haworth Labourer Baptid June ye 25th
Richd ye Son of Richd Slinger Yeaman Bapd Novr ye 1st
John ye Son of John Whitaker Farmer Bapd January 14th
Margret ye Daughr of Richd Duckitt Horse Ryder Bapd Octr ye 12th
Richd ye Son of Mary Duckit Bastard Child Baptd Octr 17th
Thos ye Son of Collumbus Ingleby Yeaman Bapd January ye 2d

1756 Burials. [C fol. 5 v.

Isabel Tennant Buried Sepr ye 27th
Thos Layland Yeaman Buried Octr ye 5th
Ann Waddilove Buried January ye 24th
Elisabeth Demain Buried April ye 8th

1757 Baptisms.

John ye Son of Robt Slinger Yeaman Bapd May ye 19th
Henry ye Son of Henry Ellis Joyner Baptd June ye 12th
George ye Son of John Petty Labourer Baptd July ye 10th
Lupton ye Son of Lupton Wrathall Farmer Baptd Augst ye 28th
John ye Son of John Constantine Yeaman Baptd Sepr ye 25th
Stephen ye Son of John Preston Farmer Febuary ye 12th
John ye Son of John Mallisson Taylor Bapd March ye 19th

Burials.

Jane Constantine Buried Septr ye 24th
Mary ye Wife of Richd Robinson Husbandman Buried Fabury ye 15th
Alice Robinson Widdow Buried March ye 16th
John ye Son of Robt Slinger Buried March ye 19th

1758 Baptisms.

Alice ye Daughr of Robt Slinger Yeaman Bapd July ye 9th
Francis ye Son of Tho. Petty Husbandman Bapd Augt ye 20th
Ellin ye Daughr of Richd Duckitt Horse Ryder Baptd Octr ye 12th
Willm ye Son of Wm Haworth Labourer Bapd Octr ye 15th
Richd ye Son of Richd Slinger Yeaman Baptid Novr ye 1st
John ye Son of John Whitaker Yeaman Baptid January ye 14th

Burials.

Margat ye Daughr of John Tennant Gentleman Buried April ye 30th
Richd Robinson Husbandman Buried May ye 19th
Richd Slinger Yeaman Buried May ye 17th
Francis Duckitt Farmer Buried Septr ye 4th
Margat ye Daughr of John Clark Farmer Buried Novr ye 1st
George ye Son of John Petty Husbandman Buried March ye 29th

## 1759 Burials.

Alice ye Daughr of Henry Brotherton Labourer Bapd July ye 22d
Margat ye Daughr of John Whitaker Yeaman Bapd Decr ye 30th
Henry the Son of Wm Slinger Yeaman Baptid January ye 13th
Matthew the Son of Henry Layland Yeaman Baptid Fabuary ye 24th
Thos ye Son of Richd Duckitt Miner Baptd March ye 4th
Dorothy the Daughtr of Henry Ellis Joyner Baptd March ye 9th

## Burials.

Wm ye Son of Wm Haworth Buried June ye 19th
Alice ye Daughr of Robt Slinger Yeaman Buried July ye 22d
Margt Needham a Poor Widdow Buried July ye 11th
Henry the Son of Wm Slinger Buried July ye 25th
Charles ye Son of Henry King Innkeeper Buried March ye 20th

## 1760 Baptisms. [C fol. 6 r.

Thos ye Son of Thos Robinson Sadler Baptd June ye 1st
Wm ye Son of Wm Haworth Bapd Septr ye 13th
Richd ye Son of John Constantine Yeaman Bapd Octr ye 5th
Emanuall ye Son of Thos Tomlinson Labourer Baptid Janury ye 4th
Wm ye Son of Robt Slinger Yeaman Baptid Janury ye 25th
Wm ye Son of Wm Simpson Miner Baptid March ye 22d

## Burials.

Mary ye Wife of Edward Robinson Buried May ye 1st
Thomas Layland Widdow Buried Fabuary ye 8th
Wm Bawdin Labourer Buried March ye 24th

## 1761 Baptisms.

Sarah ye Daughr of Miles Simpson Bapd April ye 5th
James ye Son of James Middlebrook Joyner Bapd Augt ye 2d
Ralph ye Son of Joseph Nelson Miner Baptd Nor ye 15th
Thos ye Son of John Thompson Miner Baptd April ye 25th
John ye Son of Jane Stoyles a Bastard Child Bapd April ye 26th
Richd ye Son of Wm Slinger Yeaman Baptsd May ye 12th

## Burials.

Robr Holgate Buried April ye 2d

## 1762 Baptisms.

Betty ye Daughtr of Wm Duckitt Yeaman Baptd May ye 7th
Betty ye Daughtr of Humphray Topham Yeaman Baptd June ye 29th
Laurance ye Son of Cuthbert Holyday Yeaman Baptd Augt 28th
Francis ye Son of John Duckett Labourer Baptid Octr ye 3d
Alice ye Daughter of Wm Constantine Labourer Baptid Octr ye 3d
Henry ye Son of Rich Duckitt Miner Baptid Octr ye 10th
Betty ye Daughter of Wm Simpson Labourer Baptid Octr ye 24th

## Burials.

Humphray Topham Yeaman Buried Augst ye 5th
Agnes ye Wife of Richd Robinson Miner Buried Sepr ye 29th

1763 Baptisms.

George ye Son of Robr Wilkinson Labourer Baptd April ye 26th
Hannah ye Daughr of John Whitaker Farmer Baptid July ye 17th
John ye Son of David Alderson Miner Baptid Augt ye 13th
Wm ye Son of John Duckitt Labourer Baptid Novr ye 13th
Bella ye Daughter of Richd Holgate Farmer Baptid Decr ye 12th

Burials.

Joseph Horner Labourer Buried Octr ye 22d
George ye Son of Robt Wilkinson Labourer Buried Decr ye 14th
Francis ye Son of John Duckitt Labourer Buried Decr ye 27th

1764 Baptisms. [C fol. 6 v.

Binjamin ye Son of John Tomlinson Labourer Baptid April ye 8th
Fiby ye Daughr of John Holgate Miller Baptid Decr ye 16th
Feby ye Daughr of Christr Bayley Husband Man Baptd Febuary ye 10th
Alice ye Daughr of Richd Duckitt Labourer Baptid March ye 3d
Nelly ye Daughter of Richd Holgate Farmer Baptid March ye 13th

Burials.

Catheran Horner Spinster Buried April ye 1st
Mr John Tennant of Chapel House Gentleman Buried May ye 5th
Henry Constantine Yeaman Buried January ye 21the

1765 Baptisms.

Henry ye Son of William Constantine Labor Baptd June ye 9th
Henry ye Son of Francis Ovinton Labourer Bapd June ye 20th
Ellin ye Daughr of James Middlebrough Joyner Bapd Janury ye 26th
Thos ye Son of Thos Jackman Farmer Baptid Febuary ye 2d
Henry ye Son of Henry Ovinton Yeaman Baptid Febuary ye 26th

Burials.

Thos Hawworth Labourer Buried Augut ye 11th
Elisabeth Hebdin Spinster Buried March ye 16th

[C fol. 7 r.

A Register Bill of all Baptisms and Burials had in the Chapel of Coniston in the Parish of Burnsall from March 25 in the year 1766 till March ye 25th 1767.

Henry the Son of John Constantine Yeaman was Baptized Agust the 31st by the Reverd Mr John Alcock.

Robert the Son of William Hallam Miner was baptized Agust ye 31st by the Revd Mr John Alcock.

John the Son of John Whitaker Yeaman was baptized October the 12th by the Revd Mr John Alcock.

Ann the Daughter of Richard Holdgate Farmer was baptized October the 12th by the Revd Mr John Alcock.

Edon the Daughter of John Demain Miner was Baptized Febuary the 15th by Mr John Alcock.

Burials.

Henry Ellis Joner was Buried September ye 21st by the Revd Mr William Tenant.

James Robison was bured Desember the 14 by the Rev^d^ M^r^ Mathew Knowls.
An Constantine was buried jinuary the 18 by the Rev^d^ M^r^ John Hirst.
Thomas Ducket was buried Febuary ^th^ 3 By the Rev^d^ M^r^ John Hirst.
Richard Ducket was Buried March the 11 by the Revd. M^r^ John Alcock.

A Register Bill of all the Baptisms and Burials that has been in the Chappel of Conniston in the Parish of Burnsall and County of York from March the 25^th^ in the Year of our Lord 1767 to March the 25^th^ 1768.

Burials.

Mary the Daughter of Thomas Ibbotson Labourer was Buried May the 10^th^ by the Rev^d^ Jn^o^ Alcock.

Alice the Daughter of W^m^ Constantine Labourer was Buried July the 26^th^ by the Rev^d^ M^r^ Matthew Knowles.

Henry the Son of Henry Ellis joiner was Buried November the 5^th^ by the Rev^d^ M^r^ Matthey Knowles.

Betty and Nancy the Daughters of Jn^o^ Hebdin Farmer was Buried November the 10^th^ by the Rev^d^ M^r^ Jn^o^ Hewit.

Sarah the Daughter of James Middlebrough joiner was Buried November the 15^th^ by the Rev^d^ M^r^ Matthew Knowles.

Luke Horner Farmer was Buried November 17^th^ by the Rev^d^ M^r^ Matthew Knowles.

Arabella the Daughter of Rich^d^ Ducket Labourer was Buried November the 29^th^ by the Rev^d^ M^r^ Matthew Knowles.

Susanna the Daughter of Lupton Wrathall Yeaman was Buried December 2^d^ by the Rev^d^ M^r^ Matthew Knowles.

Mary the Daughter of Rich^d^ Ducket Labourer was Buried December 15^th^ by the Rev^d^ M^r^ Matthew Knowles.

Mary the Daughter of Rich^d^ Blakey Labourer was Buried December 16^th^ by the Rev^d^ M^r^ Matthew Knowles.

William the Son of Rob^t^ Slinger Yeaman was Buried December 18^th^ by the Rev^d^ M^r^ Matthew Knowles.

Matthew the Son of Henry Leyland Yeaman was Buried December 21^th^ by the Rev^d^ M^r^ Matthew Knowles.

Edom the Daughter of Jn^o^ Demain Miner was Buried January 29^th^ by the Rev^d^ M^r^ Matthew Knowles.

Baptisms 1767. [C fol. 7 v.

Nancy the Doughter of Jn^o^ Hebdin Farmer was Baptized May 10^th^ by the Rev^d^ M^r^ Jn^o^ Alcock.

Francis the Son of Jn^o^ Ducket Farmer was Baptized May 24^th^ by the Rev^d^ Jn^o^ Hewit.

Jonathan the Son of David Alderson Farmer was Baptized July 14^th^ by the Rev^d^ M^r^ Matthew Knowles.

Isabel the Daughter of W^m^ Constantine Labourer was Baptized December 13^th^ by the Rev^d^ M^r^ Matthew Knowles.

W^m^ the Son of Rich^d^ Ducket Labourer was Baptized December 13 by the Rev^d^ M^r^ Matthew Knowles.

Jn^o^ the Son of W^m^ Ducket Yeaman was Baptized January 3^d^ by the Rev^d^ M^r^ Jn^o^ Alcock.

[Martha the Daughter of George Horrner Babtiz^d^ 9^d^ Sep 1773 by the John Alcock.]

## Baptisms in the Year 1771.

George the Son of W[m] Porter Taylor Baptised December the 15[th] 1771 by the Reverand John Alcock.

Ellin the Doughter of John Hallam Miner Baptised January the 12[th] 1772 By the Reverand Matt' Knowles.

Aprill 14[th] 1772 John and Elliz[e] the Son and Doughter of Edward Heslton Miner Baptised By the Reverand George Fletcher.

[Aprill 16[th] 1772 Easter the Douter of Jane Stoyles Babtiz[d] by M[r] Math' Knowles].

May [th] 3 1772 Christopher the Son of Eliz: Downs a Basterd Child Baptised by the Reverand John Alcock.

Alce the Doughter of Richard Heselton Cordwinder Babtized October 18[th] 1772 by the Rev[d] John Alcock.

Ellin the Doughter of Francis Ovington Burid Octob[r] 28[th] 1772 by the Rev[d] Matt[w] Knowles.

Ellin the Doughter of John Duckett Yeaman Buried Nov[r] 29[th] 1772 By the Reverand John Alcock.

Easter the Doughter of Jane Stoyles a Basterd Child Buried December th. 8 72 By the Rev[d] Matt. Knowles.

## Burials for the Year 1772.

Elin the Doughter of John Hallam Buried Jan[y] 22[d] 1772 By the Rev[d] John Alcock.

John and Eliz. the Son and Doughter of Edward Heselton Buried Aprill the 17[th] By the Rev[d] Matt[w] Knowles.

June [th] 17 1772 Alice Heselton a Widdow Buried by the Rever[d] Matt: Knowles.

John the Son of Robert Wilkinson inkeper Buried Augst the 9[th] by the Rev[d] John Alcock.

Thomas the Son of John Demain Babtized Aug[st] 30[th] by the Rev[d] John Alcock.

Mary the Doughter of George Horrner Yeaman Babtized October the 4[th] 1772 by the Reverand John Alcock.

Ellin the Doughter of Francis Ovington Labour Baptized October 4[th] 1772 by the Reverand John Alcock.

James the Son of John Duckitt Babtized Decb[r] 20 1772 by the Rev[d] John Alcock.

Conistone Chapel 1797. [D fol. 1 r.

This Marriage was solemnized between us by Banns Christopher Buckle and Ann Hudson this 7 Day of August 1797.

John Alcock Rect^r of Burnsall.

Witness Anthony Robinson — Christopher Buckle
Henry Ovington — Ann Hudson × her mark

Conistone Chapel 1797.

This Marriage after publication by Banns was solemnized in the said Chapel by the Rev^d John Wilson betwixt John Beecroft & Mary Hesleton both within the said chapelry as Witness our hands this 13^th day of December 1797. John Wilson Curate.

Witness Henry Ovington — John Beecroft × his Mark
Charls Holgate — Mary Hesleton × her Mark

John Tennant and Sarah Slinger of the Chapelry of Conistone were Married in this Chapel of Conistone with Consent of Parents this 17^th day of December in the Year of our Lord 1797 by me John Alcock Rect^r of Burnsall. This marriage was solemnised between John Tennant

In the Presence of John Middlebrouck — Sarah Slinger
Robert Hallam.

[D fol. 1 v.

Married by Licence in the Chapelry of Counistone in the Parish of Burnsall this 2^d Day of July 1803 William Eyre of Why-coller in the Forist Tr'awden & County Palantine of Lancaster farmer & Margaret Furnish of Chapel House in the Parish of Burnsall and Diocese of York by me John Alcock Rect^r of Burnsall.

Witness William Coates — William Eyre × his mark
James Airton — Margaret Furniss

Christopher Atkinson and Mary Wrider were Married in the Chapel of Conistone in the Parish of Burnsall by Banns this 12^th Day of May 1804 by me John Alcock Rect^r of Burnsall.

Witness John Leyland — Christopher Atkinson × his Mark
John Downs — Mary Wrider × her Mark

Married by Licencene in the Chapelry of Counistone in the Parish of Burnsall this 7^th Day of May 1808 William Wilson of Starbotton in the Parish of Kettlewell and Ann Shharp in the Parish of Burnsall. John Alcock Rect^r of Burnsall.

Witness William Falshaw — William Wilson
John Lodge — Ann Sharp

Married by Banns in the Chapel of Conistone this 29^th Day of August 1808 John Green and Sarah Broughton both in the Parish of Burnsall by John Alcock Rect^r of Burnsall.

Witness Thomas Bland — John Green
W^m Inman — Sarah Broughton × her Mark.

[D fol. 2 r.

Married by banns in the Chapelry of Coniston in the Parish of Burnsall this 13^th day of June 1811. Robert Wrathall of Coniston in Kettlewelldale in the Parish of Burnsall Farmer and Ann

Davis of Coniston aforesaid and Diocese of York by Me John Wilson Curate.

Witness Stephen Wrathall — Robert Wrathall
Mercy Davys — Ann Davis

William Stoils of Coniston and Alice Rathmell of Kilnsey in the Parish of Burnsall were married in this Chapel of Coniston by Banns this second Day of September 1811 by me Rich[d] Withnell Rector of Burnsall.

This Marriage was solemnized between us { The Mark × of William Stoils
The Mark × of Alice Rathmell

In the Presence of Mary Hesleton
John Ellis

Married by Licence in the Chapelry of Coniston and Parish of Burnsall this 17[th] day of Dec[r] 1812. Luke Horner of Coniston in Kettlewell-dale in the Parish of Burnsall Yeoman and Betty Downs of Coniston aforesaid and Diocese of York by Me Steph[n] Bland Minister.

Witness Will[m] Duckitt — Luke Horner
Jos. Horner — Betty Downs

---

[D fol. 3 v.

Rich[d] Constantine Dyed Sep[t] 1746 15[d] Aged 63.
Jonathan Constantine Dyed May 17[d] 1768 Aged 73.
Henry Constantine Dyed Nov[r] 23[d] 1769 Aged 80.

Baptisms. [D fol. 4 r.

Ann the Doughter of Rich[d] Blackay Labouor Baptiz[d] Deb[r] 3[d] 1768 by Rev[d] J : Alcock.

Baptizms. [D fol. 4 v.

Ann the Doughter of Rich[d] Holgate farmer Bap[d] Sep[r] 6[th] 1766 By J.A.

Rob[t] the Son of Rich[d] Holgate farmer Babtiz[d] Jan[y] 15[th] 1769 by the Rev[d] J : Alcock.

John the Son of John Duckit Labouor Babtiz[d] Jan[y] 12[d] 1769 by the Rev[d] J : Alcock.

Mary the Daughter of W[m] Ibbotson Labourer Baptized March 31[st] 1768.

Jonathan the Son of W[m] Constantine Labouor Baptiz[d] feb[r] 5[th] 1770 by J : Alcock.

Charles Son of John Duckitt Labouor Babtiz[d] April 12[d] 1770 by the Rev[d] John Alcock.

Alice the Doughter of Rob[t] Hallam miner Baptiz[d] Sep[r] 17[th] 1768 By the Rev[y] J : A.

Mary the Doughter of W[m] Clark Butcher Bap[d] Jan[y] 24[th] 1770 By R[d] J : A.

Baptizisms.

W[m] the Son of Rob[t] Hallam minor Babtiz[d] Aug[st] 27 1770 By the Rev[d] John Alcock.

W[m] Constantine Labouor Buried July 25[d] 1770 by the Rev[d] M[r] Knowels.

Charles the Son of John Duckitt Lobouor Buried Aug[st] 27[d] 1770 by J : Alcock.

Isabella the Doughter of Rich[d] Blackay Labouor Babtiz[d] Deb[r] 23[d] 1770 by J : A.

Charles the Son of Rich[d] Holgate farmer Babtiz[d] Decemb[r] 26[th] 1770 By the Rev[d] J : A.

Robert the Son of W[m] Ibbotson Labour Bap[d] feb[r] 2[d] 1770.

Ellin the Doughter of John Duckitt Labouor Babtiz'd July 6[d] 1771 by the Rev[d] J : A.

1770 Babtizisms. [D fol. 5 r.

Martha the Daughter of George Horrner Yeoman Babtized Sep[r] 9[th] 1770 By the Rev[rd] John Alcock.

George the Son of William Porter Taylor Babtized Decemb[r] 15[th] 1771 By the Rev[d] John Alcock.

Ellin the Dougter of John Hallam miner Baptiz[d] Jan[y] 12[th] 1772 By the Rev[d] Math' Knowels.

John and Ellin the Son and Doughter of Edward Heslton miner Babtiz' April 14[th] 1772 By the Rev[d] George Fletcher.

Easter the Doughter of Jane Stoyles a Basterd Child Babtiz Aprill 16[d] By the Rev[d] Math' Knowles.

Christoper the Son of Elizabeth Downes a Basterd Child Babtiz[d] May 3[th] 1772 By the Rev[d] John Alcock.

Alce the Doughter of Rich[d] Heslton Cordwinder Babtiz[d] Octob[r] 18[th] 1772 By the Rev[d] John Alcock.

Tomas the Son of John Demain Miner Babtiz' August 30[th] 1772 By the Rev[d] John Alcock.

Mary the Doughter of George Horrner Yeoman Babtiz' Octob[r] 4[th] 1772 By the Rev[d] John Alcock.

Ellin the Doughter of Fran[s] Ovington Labouor Baptiz' Octob[r] 4[th] 1772 By the Rev[d] John Alcock.

James the Son of John Duckit Labouor Babtiz' Decemb[r] 20[th] 1772 By the Rev[d] John Alcock.

Burialls.

Ellin the Doughter of John Hallam Miner Bured Jan[y] 22[th] 1772 By the Rev[d] Math Knowles.

John and Ellin the Son & Doughter of Ed : Heslton Buried Apriel 17[th] 1772 By the Rev[d] J : A.

Alice Heslton a widow Buried June 17[th] 1772 By the Rev[d] Math' Knowles.

John the Son of Rob[t] Wilkinson Inkeper Buried Aug[st] 9[th] By the Rev[d] John Alcock.

Ellin the Doughter of Fra[s] Ovington Buried Oct[r] 28[th] 1772 By the Rev[d] Math' Knowles.

Ellin the Doughter of John Duckitt Buried Nov[r] 29[th] 1772 By the Rev[d] Math' Knowles.

Easter the Doughter of Jane Stoyles Buried Deb[r] 8[th] 1772 By the Rev[d] M[w] Knowles.

Babtizisms. [D fol. 5 v.

Dolley the Doughter of W[m] Hallam miner Baptiz[d] Jan[y] 10[th] 1773 By the Rev[d] John Alcock.

Isabell the Doughter of John Mason farmer Babtiz[d] Jan[y] 17[th] 1773 By the Rev[d] John Alcock.

Thomas the Son of Rich[d] Blackay Labouor Baptiz[d] Jan[y] 31[th] 1773 By the Rev[d] John Alcock.

Martha the Doughter of Rob[t] Hallam Baptiz[d] March 21[st] 1773 By the Rev[d] John Alcock.

Rich[d] the Son of Rich[d] Holgate farmer Babtiz[d] April the 4[th] 1773 by the Rev[d] John Alcock.

Ann the Doughter of William Clarke Butcher Baptiz[d] June the 13[d] 1773 by the Rev[d] John Alcock.

Barnabas the Son of John Hallam Babtiz[d] June 27[d] 1773 by the Rev[d] John Alcock.

Sep[r] 11[d] 1773 Christop[r] Holyday Buried By the Rev[d] Matt' Knowles.

Barnabas the Son of John Hallam Buried Octob[r] 10[d] 1773 by the Rev[d] John Alcock.

Elizabeth Constantine Widow of John Constantine of Coniston Buried Octob[r] 24[th] 1773 By the Rev[d] John Alcock.

Nov[r] 21[d] 1773 Jonathan the Son of Edward Heslton Babtiz[d] by the Rev[d] John Alcock.

January 16[th] 1774 Mary the Doughter of James Press Babtiz[d] by the Rev[d] John Alcock.

feb[r] 20[d] 1774 Thomas the Son of W[m] Ibbotson Babtiz[d] by the Rev[d] John Alcock.

Ap[r] 24[d] 1774 Ann the Doughter of W[m] Clark Bucher Buried by the Rev[d] M : Knowles.

May 15[th] 1774 Robert Slinger Buried by the Rev[d] Matt. Knowles.

Sep[r] 11[th] 1774 Mathias the Son of John Hallam Bab[t] by the Rev[d] Matt. Knowles.

Sep[r] 16 1774 Tho[s] the Son of W[m] Ibbotson Babtiz[d] by the Rev[d] M[r] Alcock.

Octob[r] 6[th] 1774 Mary the Douther of Rich[d] Blackay Labour Babtiz[d] by the Rev[d] John Alcock.

Nov[r] 13[th] 1774 Nancy the Doughter of John Duckitt Babtiz[d] By the Rev[d] John Alcock.

[D fol. 6 r.

John the Son of John Demain Babtiz[d] Jan[y] 8[th] 1775 By the Rev[d] John Alcock.

Eliz[e] the Doughter of George Horrner Babtiz[d] Jan[y] 8[th] 1775 By the R[d] J : Alcock.

Peggey the Doughter of Chri[s] Pettyt Babtiz[d] Aprii 14[th] 1775 By the Rev[d] J : Alcock.

Ann the Doughter of Fran[s] Ovington Babtiz[d] Ap[r] 23[d] 1775 By M : Knowles.

W[m] the Son of W[m] Hallam Babtiz[d] May the 21[th] 1775 By the Rev[d] M : Knowles.

W[m] the Son of John Proctor Taylor Bab[d] July [th] 9 1775 By the R[d] J : Alcock.

Mirrel the Doughter of Richard Heslton Cordwinder Babtiz[d] July the 23[d] 1775 by the Rev[d] John Alcock.

Rob[t] the Son of Rob[t] Hallam Babtiz[d] Decemb[r] 31[th] 1775 By the Rev[d] John Alcock.

Jane the Doughter of Rob[t] Wrathal Babtiz[d] Jan[y] 21[st] 1776 By the Rev[d] J : A.

1755.

George Castle a Bachelor Buried Jan$^{y}$ 8$^{th}$ 1775 By the Rev$^{d}$ John Alcock.

John the Son of John Demain Buried Jan$^{y}$ $^{th}$ 22 by the Rev$^{d}$ John Alcock.

Mirell the wife of John Mallinson Taylor Buried Mar. 18$^{d}$ By J : Alcock.

Mary Slinger widow of Rob$^{t}$ Slinger Buried April 6$^{th}$ 1775 By J. Alcock.

Eliz$^{e}$ the Doughter of George Horrner Buried April 26$^{th}$ 1775 By the Rev$^{d}$ Mathew Knowels.

Alice the Wife of James Hebden Buried May the 9. 1775 By the Rev$^{d}$ M : Knowles.

M$^{rs}$ Jane Tennant Relulet of John Tennant of Chapel House Esq$^{r}$ Buried Decemb$^{r}$ 26$^{th}$ 1775 By the Rev$^{d}$ Matt. Knowles.

Ann the Wife of John Hebden Buried Jan$^{y}$ 21$^{st}$ 1776 By the Rev$^{d}$ J. A.

Thomas Demane Buried feb$^{r}$ 18$^{d}$ 1776 By the Rev$^{d}$ John Alcock.

pattey the Doughter of John Houton Bab$^{d}$ Mar. 2$^{th}$ 1776 By the Rev$^{d}$ J : Alcock.

Henry the Sun of Edmond Airtun of Chappel Lodg Babtised March 24$^{th}$ 1776 By the Riv$^{d}$ John Alcock.

Marthew the Daughter of George Horner was Buried March 24$^{th}$ 1776 By the Riv$^{d}$ John Alcock.

Mary the wife of Henry Layland Buried Ap$^{r}$ 4$^{th}$ 1776 By the Rev$^{d}$ John Alcock.

Isabell the Doughter of John Demain Babtiz$^{d}$ Ap$^{r}$ 4 1776 By the Rev$^{d}$ J : Alcock.

George the Son of Geo$^{r}$ Horrner Bab$^{d}$ Ap$^{r}$ 5$^{th}$ 1776 By the Rev$^{d}$ J : Alcock.

John the Son of John Duckit Burid Ap$^{r}$ 8$^{d}$ By the Rev$^{d}$ Matt. Knowles.

John Constantine son of Hen$^{y}$ Constantine Buri$^{d}$ July 24$^{th}$ 1776 By the Rev$^{d}$ Matt$^{w}$ Knowles.

John Vipont of Blackborn Buri$^{d}$ August 4$^{th}$ 1776 By the Rev$^{d}$ John Alcock.

Roger Ward Doctor Buried Nov$^{r}$ 17$^{th}$ 1776 By the Rev$^{d}$ John Alcock.

Alice Duckitt Buried Deb$^{r}$ 13$^{d}$ 1776 By the Rev$^{d}$ John Alcock.

[D fol. 7 r.

August 18$^{th}$ 1776 John the Son of W$^{m}$ Ibbotson Babtiz : By the Rev$^{d}$ John Alcock.

Sep$^{r}$ 22$^{d}$ Charles the Son of John Duckit Labour Bab$^{t}$ By the Rev$^{d}$ Matt. Knowles.

Mary the Doughter of Charles Duckit Babtiz$^{d}$ By the Rev$^{d}$ John Alcock.

John and Robert the Sones of John Hallam Bab$^{t}$ Aug$^{st}$ 31 By the R$^{d}$ John Alcock.

Pattey the Doughter of Richard Heslton Bab$^{z}$ Aug$^{st}$ 31 1777 by the Rev$^{d}$ John Alcock.

Elliz. the Doughter of Mary Baldwin a Basterd Child Babtiz$^{d}$ Oct$^{r}$ 19$^{th}$ By the Rev$^{d}$ Matt' Metcalf.

Ann the Doughter of W$^{m}$ Hallam miner Bab' Deb$^{r}$ 7$^{th}$ By the Rev$^{d}$ John Alcock.

Henry the Son of John Duckitt Babtiz' Novr 2d 1777 By the Revd John Alcock.

Nanncy the Doughter of John Tomling Bab' Debr 28th 1777 By the Rd John Alcock.

Wm the Son of Robt Hebden farmer Babt febr 1st 1778 By the Revd John Alcock.

Mary the Doughter of Chrisr Mallison farmer Babd febr 1st 1778 By the Revd J : Alcock.

John the Son of James Airton Blacksmith Babtizd febr 15th 1778 By the Rd J : Alcock.

Pattey the Doughter of Robt Wrathall Cordwinder Babd febr 27° 1778 By the Rd J : Alcock.

John the Son of Frans Ovington Bab' Mar' 29th 1778 By the Revd J : Alcock.

Wm the Son of John Needham miner Bab' May 24th By the Revd John Alcock.

Bellay the Doughter of Richd Blackay Bab' Augt 9th By the Revd John Alcock.

Charles the Son of Charles Duckit farmer Bab' Augst 30d By the Rd J : Alcock.

Luke the Son of Geo' Horner Bab' Sepr 13th 1778 By the Revd John Alcock.

Cuthbert Holiday of North Coat Buried December the 21th 1776 By the Revd John Alcock.

Charles the Son of John Duckitt Buried Jany 3d 1777 By the Revd Mr Sheepshanks.

John Clark of Coniston Buried Jany 12th 1777 By the Revd J : Alcock.

Isabell Holgate Burid Apr 10th 1777 By the Revd Matt' Metcalf.

William Becroft Burid May 29 1777 By the Revd Tennand Bolland.

John Winder a poor man Buried June 27th By J : Alcock 1777.

John the Son of J : Hallam Miner Burid Octr 21st By the Revd Tent Bolland.

William Ellis a poor man Burid April 4d 1778 By the Revd J : Alcock.

Agnas Holyday widow of Larrance Holyday of Kilnsay Buried April 12th 1778 By the Revd John Alcock.

James & Thos the Sons of John Middelbrouk Joyner Bab' May the 12th 1778 By the Revd Tennant Bolland.

Thos Lupton a miner Buried May 21st By the Revd Chrs Naylor 1778.

William Holgate farmer Buriad May the 27th By the Revd John Alcock 1778.

Wm the Son of Wm Ibbotson Miner Burd June 28th By the Rd John Alcock 1778.

George the Son of George Horner Burd July 5th By the Rd John Alcock 1778.

Agnes the Doughter of John Tomling Burd Augst 16d By the Rd J : Alcock.

James the Son of John Middelbrok Joiner Burid Octr 1st By Mr Naylor.

1779. [D fol. 8 r.

Mar' 14th Margret the Doughter of Wm Ibbotson Babz By the Revd J. Alcock.

Margret the Doughter of Richd Duckitt Bab' April 18th By the Revd J : Alcock.

Michael the Son of James Press Bab' April 18$^{th}$ By the Rev$^{d}$ John Alcock.

May 9$^{th}$ Richard the Son of John Duckit Bap$^{z}$ by the Rev$^{d}$ John Alcock.

Isabel the Daughter of Rob$^{t}$ falshaw Bab' May 16$^{d}$ By the R$^{d}$ John Alcock.

Mary the Doughter of John Tomlin Bab' May 16$^{d}$ By the R$^{d}$ John Alcock.

Stepehen the Son of John Medelbrouf Joyner Bab' July 18$^{d}$ By the Rev$^{d}$ John Alcock.

John the Son of Charles Duckit Bab' July 28$^{th}$ By the Rev$^{d}$ John Alcock.

James the Son of John Hallam Miner Bab' Oct 3$^{th}$ By the Rev$^{d}$ M$^{r}$ Johnson.

Ann the Doughter of James Airton Blacksmith Bab' Oct$^{r}$ 10$^{th}$ By the R$^{d}$ M$^{r}$ Johnson.

Christopher the Son of Tho$^{s}$ Ibbotson Labour Bab' Deb$^{r}$ 5$^{th}$ By the Rev$^{d}$ John Alcock.

1780.

William the Son of Agnas Beckwith a Basterd Child Bab' Ja$^{y}$ 29 by the R$^{d}$ J : A.

Mary the Doughter of James Middelbrouk Joyner Bab' June 11$^{th}$ By the R$^{d}$ J : Alcock.

John the Son of Robert Halam Miner Bab' June 16$^{th}$ By the Rev$^{d}$ John Alcock.

Christopher the Son of Chris' Mallison Bab' July 2$^{th}$ By the Rev$^{d}$ John Alcock.

James the Son of James Prest Babtiz' August 13$^{th}$ By the Rev$^{d}$ John Alcock.

Grace the Doughter of Rich$^{d}$ Blackay Bab$^{t}$ Aug$^{st}$ 27 : By the Rev$^{d}$ J : Alcock.

Nancy the Doughter of Rich$^{d}$ Heslton Bab' Sep$^{r}$ 4$^{th}$ by the R$^{d}$ J : A :

1781.

Thomasin the Doughter of George Horner Bab' Ja$^{y}$ 7$^{th}$ By the R$^{d}$ J : A.

William the Son of W$^{m}$ Ibbotson miner Bab' April the 1st by the R$^{d}$ John Alcock.

Dorathy the Doughter of Tho$^{s}$ Hugison Bab' July 8$^{th}$ By the Rev$^{d}$ John Alcock.

1779.

Tho$^{s}$ the Son of John Middlebrouf Burid Mar. 23$^{th}$ By the Rev$^{d}$ Ch$^{r}$ Naylor.

Alice the Doughter of Rob$^{t}$ Hallam Miner Buri$^{d}$ April 18$^{th}$ By the R$^{d}$ J : Alcock.

Sarah Lawson of Chapel House Buri$^{d}$ May 16$^{d}$ By the R$^{d}$ John Alcock.

Robert the Son of W$^{m}$ Hallam miner Burid May 19$^{th}$ R$^{d}$ Chr$^{s}$ Naylor.

Michail the Son of James Press Buri$^{d}$ May 25$^{th}$ By the Rev$^{d}$ Chris$^{r}$ Naylor.

W$^{m}$ the Son of John Needam Miner Buried June 7$^{th}$ By the Rev$^{d}$ John Alcock.

John Mallison Taylor Buried July 24$^{th}$ By the Rev$^{d}$ John Alcock.

1780.

Richard Horrner Skiner Buried Jan$^{y}$ 27$^{th}$ By the Rev$^{d}$ John Alcock.

Francies Topham from Blackb$^{n}$ Buried June 16$^{th}$ By the Rev$^{d}$ J: Alcock.

Rich$^{d}$ the Son of John Duckitt Burid Sep$^{r}$ 4$^{th}$ By the R$^{d}$ J: Alcock.

Mary the Doughter of James Middelbrouk Jun$^{r}$ Bur$^{d}$ Oct$^{r}$ 29$^{th}$ J: A.

Ann Winder a poor Woman Buried Nov$^{r}$ 9$^{th}$ By the R$^{d}$ J: Alcock.

1781.

Ann the wife of Tho$^{s}$ Ibbotson Buri$^{d}$ June 27$^{d}$ By the R$^{d}$ John Alcock.

Isabela the Doughter of Rob$^{t}$ Wrathal Burid Oct$^{r}$ 31$^{st}$ By the Rev$^{d}$ J: Alcock.

Elizabeth Robinson a poor woman Buri$^{d}$ Jan$^{y}$ 5$^{d}$ By the R$^{d}$ John Alcock.

1782.

John Tatterson Burid Jan$^{y}$ 18$^{th}$ By the Rev$^{d}$ John Alcock.

Henry Layland Burid feb$^{r}$ 1$^{st}$ By the Rev$^{d}$ John Alcock.

John Topham from Blackburn Burid March 17$^{d}$ By J. Alcock.

Margrat Topham from Blackburn Bured Deb$^{r}$ 6$^{th}$ By the R$^{d}$ J. Alcock.

Ann Clark widow of John Clark of Conistone Burid Deb$^{r}$ 13$^{th}$ by J. A.

1781. [D fol. 9 r.

James the Son of James Airton Blacksmith Bab' Aug$^{st}$ 11$^{th}$ By the Rev$^{d}$ John Alcock.

Margret the Daughter of Roger Broughton Bap' Sep$^{r}$ 2$^{d}$ By J: A.

jemima the Doughter of Marcy Baldwin a Basterd Child Bap' Sep$^{r}$ 23$^{d}$

Nelley the Doughter of John Hallam Miner Bap' Sep$^{r}$ 23$^{d}$ the Rev$^{d}$ J: A.

Rob$^{t}$ the Son of W$^{m}$ Hallam Miner Bap' Sep$^{r}$ 23$^{d}$ By the Rev$^{d}$ J: Alcock.

Isabella the daughter of Rob$^{r}$ Wrathall Cordwainer baptiz'd October 7$^{th}$ by J. Wilson.

John the Son of John Duckitt Labour Bap' Nov. 25 By the R$^{d}$ John Alcock.

Tho$^{s}$ the Son of Jos: Lupton Miner Bap' Deb$^{r}$ 30$^{th}$ By the R$^{d}$ J: Alcock.

1782.

May $^{th}$ 5 Tho$^{s}$ the Son of Tho$^{s}$ Ibbotson Labour Bap$^{t}$ By the R$^{d}$ J. Alcock.

Susana the Doughter of John Tennant Labour Bap$^{t}$ Aug$^{st}$ 4$^{th}$ By the R$^{d}$ J: A.

Sarah the Daughter of John Tennant Labour Bap$^{t}$ Oct$^{r}$ 6$^{th}$ By the R$^{d}$ J: A.

Margret the Doughter of Rob$^{t}$ Wrathal Bap$^{t}$ Octo$^{r}$ 27$^{d}$ By the R$^{d}$ J: A.

Sarah the Doughter of James Middelbouk Jun$^{r}$ Bap$^{d}$ Oct$^{r}$ 27$^{d}$ by J: A.

Richard the Son of Rich^d^ Heslton Cordwainer Bap' Deb^r^ 8^th^ by the R^d^ John Alcock.

W^m^ the Son of Rich^d^ Blackey Labour Bap' Deb^r^ 22^d^ By the Rev^d^ J: Alcock.

1783.

Bettey the Doughter of Richard Duckitt Labour Bab' Jan^y^ 29^th^ By the R^d^ J: A.

April 6^th^ Henry the Son of Tho^s^ Huginson Bap' By the R^d^ J: Alcock.

May 11^d^ W^m^ the Son of Jos: Lupton minor Bab' By the R^d^ J: Alcock.

1783. [D fol. 10 r.

March 2^th^ John the Son of John Duckit Labour Buried By the R^d^ John Alcock.

Rebeca the Doughter of John Duckit Labour Bap' Aug^t^ 17^d^ By R^d^ J: A^k.^

John the Son of George Horner Bap' Sep^r^ 14^th^ By the R^d^ J: Alcock.

Sarah the Doughter of Roger Brouton Bap' Nov^r^ 30^th^ By the R^d^ J: Alcock.

Christopher the Son of Ann Pettey a Basterd Child Bap' Deb^r^ 25^th^ By the R^d^ J: Alcock.

Thomas the Son of Ch^r^ Mallison Labour Bap' Deb^r^ 25^th^ By the R^d^ Jo^n^ Alcock.

1784.

Mary the Doughter of John Tennant Labour Bap' May 16^th^ By J: A:

Bettey the Doughter of Tho^s^ Ibbotson Miner Bap' July 25^d^ By R^d^ J: Alcock.

Thomas the Son of John Pettey Jun^r^ farmer Bap' Augst 29^d^ By R^d^ J: Alcock.

April 6^th^ 1785 received the Duty thus far for Sarah Harrison Sub collector p. Sam^l^ Crowther.

Nov^r^ the 10^th^ Betty the Daughter of Tho^s^ Demain Farmer Baptz^d^ by the Rev^d^ John Alcock.

Richard the Son of John Stoyles Poper Bap' Deceb^r^ 19^th^ By the R^d^ J: Alcock.

1785.

Martha the Doughter of Rich^d^ Heslton Cordwainer Baptiz^d^ March 6^th^ By the Rev^d^ John Alcock.

Jane the Doughter of James Prest Labour Bap' March 13^th^ By the J: A.

Rich^d^ the Son of W^m^ Ibbotson Minor Bap' Ap^l^ 3^d^ By the Rev^d^ J: A.

Margrat the Doughter of Jos' Lupton miner Bap' May 29^th^ By the Rev^d^ J: Alcock.

Rebecca the Doughter of Rich^d^ Blackay Labour Bap' June 14^d^ By the Rev^d^ J: Alcock.

Susana the Doughter of Rob^t^ Wrathal Cordwainer Bap' July 20^d^ By J: A.

Rec^d^ the Duty thus far.

Ellin the Doughter of Jas Middelbrouk Joyner Bap^t^ Oct^r^ 16^th^ By the R^d^ J: A.

1786.

Jane the Doughter of John Pettey farmer Bap' April 14d By the Revd J : Alcock.

Sarah the Doughter of Henry Constantine Gentelman Bapt April 30d By J : A.

Ann the Doughter of Lawc Holiday Yeoman May 6 Bap'.

Jane the Doughter of Thos Ibbotson a poper Bap' June 25d By Rd J : A.

Thomas the Son of John Leyland Yeoman Bap' Sepr 7th By Rd J : A.

Edward the Son of Jas Prest minor Bap' Octr 1d By Rd J : A.

Thomas the Son of Geo : Horner Yeoman Bap' Debr 31d By the Rd J : Alcock.

1787.

Nelley the Doughter of Roger Broughton Miner Bap' Jay 7th By the Rd J : Alcock.

Betty the Doughter of Anty Downes farmer Bap' Jay 11th By the Rd J : Alcock.

Richd the Son of Richd Blackay poper Bap' febr 6th By the Rd J : Alcock.

Jane the Doughter of John Stoyles a poper Bap' Mar' 4th By the Rd J : Alcock.

Abram the Son of John Tennant Labour Bap' Mar' 18th By the Rd J : Alcock.

John the Son of Emanuel Tomlinson Cordwaner Bap' April 6th By Rd J : A.

Marey the Doughter of Joseph Lupton Miner Aprel 14th By Rd : J : A.

Anthy the Son of Michal Downs farmer Bap' June 10th By the Rd J : A.

Francis the Son of John Needham minor Bap' Augst 5th By the Rd J : A.

Thomas the Son of John Middelbrouk Joyner Bap' Augst 5d by the Rd J : Alcock.

Mary the Doughter of Wm Kitching farmer Bap' Octr 21st By the Rd J : Alcock.

Paid to the 1st of Octr 1787.

1784 Burials. [D fol. 11 r.

January 27th Thomas the Son of John Pettey farmer Burid By the Rd J. Alcock.

Thos Ibotson Poper Buri'd Febry 16th By the Rd J : Alcock.

Richard the Son of Richard Hasleton Cordwainer Burd Feby 18 By the rd John Alcock.

Margrat the Douter of Willm Ibotson Miner Burd March the 5th By the Reverend John Alcock.

Christopher the Son of Thos Ibotson Miner Burd March the 6th by the Reverend John Alcock.

Ann the Doughter of Wm Hallam Miner Burd March 14th By the Rd J : A.

Thomas Huginson Poper Burid April 20d By the Rd John Alcock.

Wm Horner from Pudsay Burd May 6th By the Revd John Alcock.

Jane the Wife of Chrisr Mallison Labour Burd June 22d By the Rd J : Alcock.

Aprill 6th 1785 received the contents thus for Sarah Harrison Sub distributor p. Saml Crowther.

Ruth the Wife of James Ellis Burd Oct the 8th By the Rd J : Alcock.

1785.

Thos the Son of Chrs Mallison Labour Burid Jany 20d By the Rd John Alcock.

Ann Holland Servant to Mr Tennant of Chapel-house Burid Jeny 27d By the Revd John Alcock.

Ann the Doughter of Rd Blackay Burid febr 4d By the Rd J. A.

Robt Hallam Poper Miner Burid June 19th By the Revd J : Alcock.

Mary the Wife of John Tompson Burid July 26d By the Revd J : Alcock.

Rebeca the Doughter of Richd Blackay Pauper Burd Oct. 23d By the Rd J : Alcock.

Chrisr Malison Taylor Burid Debr 23th By the Revd J : Alcock.

William Duckitt Yeoman Burid Debr 29th By the Revd J : Alcock.

1786.

Thomas the Son of Robt Tatterson Burid Jany 8th By the Revd J : Alcock.

Jane the wife of Chrisr Mallison Taylor Burd Jay 30d By the Revd J : Alcock.

Robert Stonay Horse Doctor Burd July 9th By the Rd J. Alcock.

Thos Ibbotson poper Buried Octr 1st By the Rd J : Alcock.

Recd the Contents for Burials & Chris to Ocr 1st 1786.

1787.

Jane the Doughter of Ths Ibbotson poper Burd Jany 5th By the Rd J : A.

Thomas Riplay a poper Buried febr 6th By the Rd J. Alcock.

Michal Dowus farmer Buried Mar. 29d By the Rd J. Alcock.

Anna Vipont from Blackburn Burd Aprl 16 By the Rd J : Alcock.

Betty Topham for Blackburn Burd June 15d By the Rd J : Alcock.

Mrs Charlote Tennant Chapel-House Burd Augst 2nd By the Rd J : Alcock.

Lawrance Holyday Northcoat Yeoman Buried Augst 23th By the Rd J : Alcock.

Paid to the 1st of Octr 1787.

1788.

James Wrathal a Infant Buried Augst 10th By the Rd J : A.

Ann Demane a poor woman Burid Augst 14d By the Revd J : Alcock.

1788. [D fol. 11 v.

Ann Constantine from Hebden Burid Debr 27th By Rd J : Alcock.

1789.

Thomas Hebdin a poper Burid March 1st By Rd John Alcock.

Nancy the Doughter of John Stoyles a poper Burd June 25th By the Rd John Alcock.

Paid to the 26th Day of Octr 1789.

John Hebden a poper Burid Novr 12d By the Revd John Alcock.

1790.

William Clark a poper Buried Jany 3th By the Revd John Alcock.

Martha Horner widdow Burd Jany 15th By the Revd John Alcock.

Isabel Tomlison Spinster Burid febr 2d By the Revd J : Alcock.
Ann Cooke a poper Burid febr 4th By the Revd J : Acock.
Ellin Constantine Widdow Burid febr 6th By the Revd J : Alcock.
Henry the Son of William Horner Burd May 5th By the Rd J : Alcock.
John Tennant of Chapel-House Esqr Burd June 1st By the Rd J : Alcock.
Mary Beckwith a poper Buried July 18d By the Red J. Alcock.

1791.

Francis the Son of John Needham Burd April 21st By Rd J : Alcock.
Christopher Mallison Labour Burd Octr 1st By Rd J : Alcock.
Octr 1791.

1792.

Mary the Wife of James Middelbrough Joiner a poper Burid Mar' 27d By the Rd John Alcock.
John Pettey farmer Burd May 21st By the Rd J : A.
Dorithy Brown a Servant Burid May 23d By Rd J : A.
Jane Constantine Spinster Burid August 23d By Rd J : A.
John the Son of Jonathan Waddington Burd Augst 26th By Rd J : A.
Mary the Wife of John Stoyles a poper Bd Nov. 12d By Rd J : A.

1793.

jamima the Doughter of John Stoyles a poper Burd Mar' 3d By Rd J : A.
Bettey the Doughter of Grace Ibbotson poper Burid Mar' 6d By J : A.
Sarah the Doughter of John Tennant poper Burid May 9th By J : A.
Elizabeth the Wife of Tennant Becroft Burd May 16d By J. A.
Mary the Wife of Robt Wrathal Farmer Bured Augst 11d By Rd J. A.
William Holyday Yeoman Burid Decbr 25th By the Rd J. A.

1794.

Robert Tennant Gentelman Bured January 31th By Rd J. A.
Dorathy Lupton a poper Burid febr the 2d By Rd J : A.
Tennant Becroft Yeoman Burd Mar 31st By the Rd J : A.
Henry the Son of Thos Hugeson a poper Burd Apr 8th Rd J : A.
Peggey the wife of Jos' Lupton a poper Burd May 7d Rd J. A.
Elizabeth the Widow of Thos Riplay a poper Burd May 21st By J. A.
Jane the wife of Robt Tennant Esqr of Chapel House Burd Debr 27d J. A.

1795.

John Holgate Miller Bured January 31st By the Revd J : A.
Elize Widow of Wm Duckett Burid March 30th Rd J. A.
Robert Tatterson Labour Burid Sepr 6th Rd J : A.
Henry the Son of John Leyland Burd Novr 18th J. A.

1788. [D fol. 12 r.

January 20th Hannah the Doughter of Richd Haselton Cordwainer Bapt By the Revd J : Alcock.
Mary the Doughter of John Pettey farmer Bap' febr 3d By Rd J : A.
Christopher the Son of Richd Duckitt Labour Bap' Mar' 9th By Rd J : A.
Mary the Doughter of John Layland Yeaman Bap' Aprl 13d By Rd J : A.
John the Son of Sarah Hudson a Basterd Bap' July 6d By Rd J : A.

James the Son of Rob^t^ Wrather Cordwaner Bap' Aug^st^ 5^th^ By R^d^ J : A.
Ann the Doughter of James Prest Miner Bap' Aug^st^ 5^th^ By R^d^ J : A.
Martha the Daughter of H. Constantine Bap^t^ Aug^t^ 17 By R^d^ J : A.
Tho^s^ the Son of Henry Carlisle Bap^t^ Aug^st^ 31^d^ By R^d^ J : Wislon.
Bella the Doughter of Joseph Tennant Bap' Sep^r^ 1^st^ J : A.
John the Son Michel Downes farmer Bap' Sep^r^ 7^th^ By R^d^ J : A.

Paid to the 26^th^ Day of Oct^r^ 1788.

Jane the Doughter of Jane Bradlay a Basterd Child Bap^d^ Deb^r^ 14^th^ J. A.

Stephen the son of George Horne, Yeoman Bap' Deb^r^ 27^d^ By R^d^ J : Alcock.

1789.

Ann the Doughter of Anth' Downs farmer Bap' Mar' 22^d^ By R^d^ J : Alcock.

Nancy the Doughter of John Stoyles Bap' Ap^r^ 10^d^ By R^d^ J : Alcock.

Hannah the Daughter of Emanuel Tomlinson Cordwainer Bap^t^ April 30^th^ By J : Alcock.

Hen^y^ the Son of John Thomlinson Baptised Aug^t^ 16^th^ by Rev^d^ John Alcock.

Paid to the 26^th^ Day of Oct^r^ 1789.

Sarah the Daughter of Jn^o^ Tennant Labourer Baptised Octb^r^ 26^th^ by the Rev^d^ J : A.

Robert the Son of W^m^ Anderson of Chapel Lodge Hinde Bap' Deb^r^ 6^th^ By the R^d^ J : Alcock.

Betty the Doughter of Henry Carlisle Inkeper Bap' Deb^r^ 25^th^ By the R^d^ John Alcock.

1790.

Bettey the Doughter of Chris^r^ Atkinson Bap' Jan^y^ 10^th^ By the R^d^ J : Alcock.

Margrey the Doughter of Bettey Duckit a Basterd Child Bap' Jan^y^ 31^th^ J : A.

Robert the Son of James Airton Blacksmith Bap' Jan^y^ 31^th^ R^d^ J : Alcock.

Peggy the Doughter of John Pettey farmer Bap' Mar' 28^th^ By R^d^ J : Alcock.

Nancy the Doughter of James Prest Miner Bap' May 20^d^ By R^d^ J : Alcock.

Ann the Doughter of John Middelbrouk Joiner Bap' May 28^st^ By R^d^ J : Alcock.

William the Son of John Stoyles a poper Bap' June 3^th^ By R^d^ J : Alcock.

John the Son of Joseph Lupton Miner Bap' July 10^th^ By R^d^ J : Alcock.

John the Son of John Leyland Yeoman Bap' July 15^th^ By the R^d^ J : Alcock.

Thomas the Son of Jn^o^ Cockson Yeoman Bap^d^ Octb^r^ 7^th^ By the Rev^d^ Jn^o^ Alcock.

Paid to the 26^th^ Day of Oct^r^ 1790.

Jonathan Son of H. Constantine Bap^tz^ Nov^r^ 10^d^ Rev^d^ Jn^o^ Alcock.

1791.

Anthony Son of H$^{y}$ Carlisle Bap$^{t}$ Jan$^{y}$ 2$^{d}$ Rev$^{d}$ John Alcock.
Thomas Son of Michal Downs farmer Bap' Jan$^{y}$ 22$^{d}$ B Rev$^{d}$ J : A.
Robert the Son of Nancy Middelbrouk a Baserd Child Bap' Mar 25$^{th}$ J : A.
Mary the Doughter of Emanel Tomlinson Bap' April 10$^{th}$ J : A.
Peggey the Doughter of John Tompson Labour Bap' Sep$^{r}$ 6$^{d}$ By R$^{d}$ J. A.

Oct$^{r}$ 1790. Paid to 1791. Oct$^{r}$ 1$^{st}$

1792. [D fol. 12 v.

Isabel the Doughter of Chris$^{r}$ Atkinson Labour Bap' May 4$^{th}$ By R$^{d}$ J. A.

1796.

Mary the Doughter of W$^{m}$ Wrathall Bap' May 27$^{d}$ J. Alcock.

1792.

Keaty the Doughter of Jos. Lupton a poper Bap' Sep$^{r}$ 2$^{d}$ By R$^{d}$ J. A.
Mary the Doughter of Sarah Hudson Basterd Child Bap' Sep$^{r}$ 2$^{d}$ R$^{d}$ J. A.
James the Son of Pegey Mattack Bastard Child Bap' Deb$^{r}$ 2$^{d}$ R$^{d}$ J. A.

1793.

Janeuary 6$^{th}$ Margret the Doughter of Agnas Knowles a Basterd Child & poper Bap' By R$^{d}$ J. A.
John the Son of Adam Harker Lead Miner Bap' June 2$^{d}$ J. A.
July 12$^{d}$ Stephen the Son of Michiel Downes Labour Bap' By the R$^{d}$ J. A.
Tattersall Eglin the Son of John Tompson Labour' Bap' Aug$^{st}$ 28$^{th}$ J. A.

Paid from Oct$^{r}$ 1792—to Oct$^{r}$ 1793.

Jinny the Daughter of Henry Carlile Innkeeper Bap$^{d}$ Oc$^{r}$ 20$^{th}$ by J. A.

1794.

John the Son of Jonathan Wadington Stone Mason Bap$^{d}$ Aug$^{st}$ 6 By J. A.
Mary the Daughter of Stephen Wrathall Bap$^{d}$ Aug$^{t}$ 19$^{th}$ farmer.
William the Son of John Cockson Bap' Sep$^{r}$ 7$^{th}$ R$^{d}$ J. A. Yeoman.
Stephen the Son of Edward Hargraves Labour Bap' Oct$^{r}$ 5$^{d}$ J. A.
Nancy the Daughter of John Ellison Yeoman Bab' Nov' 10$^{th}$ J. A.

1795.

Jenney the Doughter of John Leyland Yeoman Bap' April 1$^{st}$ J. A.
John the Son of W$^{m}$ Duckitt farmer Bap' April 19$^{th}$ J. A.
John Ellis Hudson the Son of Sarah Hudson a Basterd Bap' May 14$^{th}$ By R$^{d}$ J. A.
Hannah Agar Bap' Sep$^{r}$ 21$^{st}$ By the Rev$^{d}$ J : Alcock.
Ellin the Daughter of Rich$^{d}$ Duckitt Labour Bap' Nov$^{r}$ 17$^{th}$ J. A.
John the Son of John Pettey farmer Bap' Deb$^{r}$ 5$^{th}$ J. A.

1796.

Mary the Doughter of Jos' Tennant Bap' May 13$^{d}$ J. A.
John the Son of John Whitaker Yeoman Bap' Deb$^{r}$ 4$^{d}$ J. A.
Elizabeth the Doughter of Rich$^{d}$ Duckit Labour Bap' Deb$^{r}$ 7$^{th}$ J. A.
Isabel the Daughter of James Ellis Joynr Bap' Deb$^{r}$ 7$^{th}$ By J. A.

1798.

James the Son of James Ellis Joynr Bap$^{d}$ feb 4$^{d}$ R$^{d}$ John Wilson.
Margrett the Doughter of John Whitaker Bap' April 28$^{d}$ J.A.
William the son of William Wrathal farmer Bap June 30$^{th}$ By the rev$^{d}$ J. Alcock.

1791. [D fol. 13 r.

Margret the Doughter of Ellin Beckwith a Basterd Child Bap' Oct$^{r}$ 28$^{th}$ J. A.
Bettey the Doughter of John Pettey farmer Bap' Nov$^{r}$ 29$^{th}$ J. A.
Henry the Son of John Ellison Farmer Bap' Deb$^{r}$ 20$^{th}$ J. A.

1792.

Henry the Son of John Leyland Yeoman Bap' June 2$^{d}$ By the R$^{d}$ J. A.
John the Son of Jonathan Waddington Stone Mason Bap' Aug$^{t}$ 7$^{d}$ By the R$^{d}$ J. A.

1792 Paid from Oct$^{r}$ 91—to Oct$^{r}$ 1792.

1797.

May y$^{e}$ 22$^{d}$ Charles Agar Baptized by John Alcock.
August y$^{e}$ 9 Isabella the Daughter of John Ellison Yeaman Bap$^{d}$ this 9$^{th}$ of Aug$^{t}$ by John Alcock.
Sep$^{r}$ 29$^{th}$ Thomasine the Daughter of M$^{r}$ John Leyland Yeoman Bap.
Oct$^{r}$ y$^{e}$ 8$^{th}$ Ellin Jakes Brown Daughter Eligitimate Bap$^{t}$ by John Alcock.
Oct$^{r}$ y$^{e}$ 22$^{d}$ Alice Petty the Daughter of John Petty Bap$^{t}$ by J : Alcock.
Deb$^{r}$ 25$^{d}$ William the Son of John Downs farmer Bap' By the Rev$^{d}$ John Alcock.

1798.

March 13$^{th}$ James the Son of Francis Haseltine of Kilnsey Husbandman Bapt$^{d}$ by J : Alcock.
*John [Robert] the Son of John Tennant of Conistone Husbandman Bap$^{d}$ March y$^{e}$ 16$^{th}$ by J : Alcock Rect$^{r}$

1798. [D fol. 13 v.

Mathew the Son of John Beecroft Labour Bap' Sep$^{r}$ 23$^{d}$ By the Rev$^{d}$ J. A.
Stephen the Son of Stephen Wrathal farmer Bap' Oct$^{r}$ 25$^{th}$ By the R$^{d}$ J. A.

1799.

John the Son of John Tennant Labou$^{r}$ Bap$^{d}$ Oct$^{r}$ 4$^{th}$ By Rev$^{d}$ J. Alcock.
Henry the Son of James Ellis Joyner Bap$^{d}$ Oct$^{r}$ 27$^{th}$ By Rev$^{d}$ J. Wilson.
William the Son of Christopher Atkinson Labou$^{r}$ Bap$^{d}$ Dec$^{r}$ 6$^{th}$ By R$^{d}$ J. A.

1800.

Walter the Son of John Downs Yeaman Bap$^{d}$ Feb$^{y}$ 23$^{d}$ By Rev$^{d}$ J. A.
Robert the Son of William Wrathal farmer Bap$^{d}$ Mar$^{h}$ 24$^{th}$ By the Rev$^{d}$ John Alcock.
Mary the Doughter of John Whitaker Yeaman Bap$^{d}$ June 26$^{st}$ by the Rev$^{d}$ J. Alcock.

---

* Corrected to Robert.

William the Son of Stephen Wrathal farmer Bap$^{d}$ Sep$^{r}$ 14$^{th}$ By R$^{d}$ J. Alcock.
Francis the Son of Francis Hesleden farmer Bap$^{d}$ Octo$^{r}$ 14$^{th}$ By Rev$^{d}$ John Alcock.

1801.

Lantt the Son of John Becroft Labou$^{r}$ Bap$^{d}$ Feb$^{y}$ 6$^{st}$ By Rev$^{d}$ John Alcock.
John the Son of Henry Whitaker Yeaman Bap$^{d}$ Mar$^{h}$ 23$^{rd}$ By Rev$^{d}$ John Alcock.
Joseph the Son of James Ellis Joyner Bap$^{d}$ Mar$^{h}$ 29$^{th}$ By the Rev$^{d}$ John Alcock.
Ellin the Doughter of John Ibbotson Labour$^{r}$ Bap$^{d}$ Oct$^{r}$ 4$^{th}$ by the Rev$^{d}$ J. A.

1802.

Elinor the Doughter of James Ellis Joyner Bap$^{d}$ March 21$^{st}$ By the Rev$^{d}$ John Alcock.
Elizabeth the Doughter of John Tennant Labour$^{r}$ Bap$^{d}$ April 4$^{th}$ By the Rev$^{d}$ John Alcock.
John the Son of John Downs Yeaman Bap$^{d}$ May 2$^{nd}$ by Rev$^{d}$ J. A.
Richard the Son of Grace Blaco Basterd Child Bap$^{d}$ May 8$^{th}$ By the Rev$^{d}$ John Alcock.
Elizabeth the Doughter of John Ellison Farmer Bap$^{d}$ May 30$^{th}$ by Rev$^{d}$ J. A.
John the Son of William Wrathall Farmer Bap$^{d}$ July 4$^{th}$ by Rev$^{d}$ J. W.
Ann the Doughter of Francis Haselton Farmer Bap$^{d}$ Novb$^{r}$ 14$^{th}$ by Rev$^{d}$ J. Alcock.
Henry the Son of Christopher Mason Labou$^{r}$ Bap$^{d}$ Novb$^{r}$ 28$^{th}$ by Rev$^{d}$ J. Alcock.

1803.

Ephraim the Son of James Ellis Joyn$^{r}$ Bap$^{d}$ March 13$^{th}$ by the Rev$^{d}$ J. Alcock.
Alx$^{r}$ the Son of Ellin Beckworth a Basterd Child Bap$^{d}$ Aug$^{st}$ 14$^{th}$ by R$^{d}$ J. Alcock.
Francis the son of Robert Wilson Lobour$^{r}$ Bap$^{d}$ Octo$^{r}$ 30$^{th}$ by R$^{d}$ J. A.
John the Son of John Downs Yeaman Bap$^{d}$ Nov$^{br}$ 3$^{d}$ by R$^{d}$ J. Alcock.

1804.

Hannah the Daughter of Harman Trueman Innkeeper Bap$^{d}$ Feb$^{y}$ 19$^{th}$ by the Rev$^{d}$ John Alcock.

1796. [D fol. 14 r.

Elizabeth Johnson a poper Bur$^{d}$ feb$^{r}$ 26$^{th}$ By the Rev$^{d}$ J. Alcock.
Charles Holgate farmer Bur$^{d}$ April 14$^{th}$ By the Rev$^{d}$ J. Alcock.
Jane the Wife of Tho$^{s}$ Tomlinson Labour Bur$^{d}$ June 7$^{th}$ By the R$^{d}$ J. Alcock.
Francis Ovington Labour Burid July 3$^{d}$ By the R$^{d}$ John Alcock.
Elizabeth the Widdow of Rob$^{t}$ Tatterson Bur$^{d}$ July 27$^{d}$ By the R$^{d}$ J : Alcock.
William Hallam a poper Bur$^{d}$ Oct$^{r}$ 15$^{th}$ By the R$^{d}$ J : Alcock.
John Cockson Yeoman Bur$^{d}$ Deb$^{r}$ 25$^{th}$ By the Rev$^{d}$ J. Alcock.

1797.

Henry the Son of James Ellis Bur$^{d}$ April 26$^{d}$ By the R$^{d}$ J. Alcock.
Ann the Widdow of Cutherbert Holyday Bur$^{d}$ June $^{th}$ 17 By the R$^{d}$ J : Wilson.
Betty the Widow of Michel Downs Bur$^{d}$ July 1$^{st}$ By R$^{d}$ J. Wilson.

1798.

John Whitaker Yeoman Bure$^{d}$ May 26$^{d}$ By the R$^{d}$ J. Alcock.
John the Son of Jos' Lupton Labour Buir$^{d}$ Octo$^{r}$ 18$^{d}$ By the R$^{d}$ J. A.
James Middelbrouk Joyner Buri$^{d}$ Octob$^{r}$ 25$^{d}$ By the R$^{d}$ J. A.

1799.

Mary the widdow of John Pettey Bur$^{d}$ April first By the Rev$^{d}$ J. A.
Ann the Doughter of John Elison Farmer Bap' April 7$^{th}$ By the R$^{d}$ J. A.
Steven the Son of Steven Wrathal [farmer] Bure$^{d}$ June 16$^{th}$ By the Rev$^{d}$ J. Alcock.
George Frankland Labour Bure$^{d}$ Agust 28$^{d}$ By the Rev$^{d}$ J. Alcock.
Margarat the Widdow of William Clark a poper Buri$^{d}$ november 14$^{th}$ By the Rev$^{d}$ John Alcock.

1800.

Henry Constantine Yeaman Buri$^{d}$ Feb$^{y}$ 10$^{th}$ By the Rev$^{d}$ J. Wilson.
James the Son of Francis Hasleton Labour$^{r}$ Buri$^{d}$ Mar$^{h}$ 9$^{th}$ By the Rev$^{d}$ John Alcock.
Mary the Doughter of John Tennant Labour Buri$^{d}$ April 4$^{th}$ By R$^{d}$ J. A.
Jonathan Wadington Mason Burid June 26$^{st}$ By the Rev$^{d}$ John Alcock.
Susanah Dixon Gentlewoman Buri$^{d}$ Novb$^{r}$ 2$^{d}$ By the Rev$^{d}$ John Alcock.

1801.

Mary the Doughter of Christopher Atkinson Opoper Buri$^{d}$ April 14$^{th}$ by the Rev$^{d}$ John Alcock.
James Smith Opoper Buri$^{d}$ May 11$^{th}$ by the Rev$^{d}$ John Alcock.
Henry Ovington Yeaman Burid Oct$^{r}$ 14$^{th}$ By the Rev$^{d}$ John Alcock.

1802.

Richard Hesleton Cordwinder Burid Jan$^{y}$ 2$^{nd}$ by Rev$^{d}$ John Alcock.
Richard the Son of Grace Blaco a Basterd Child Buri$^{d}$ May 12$^{th}$ By the Revd John Alcock.
Elizabeth the Doughter of Christopher Atkinson Buri$^{d}$ September 9$^{th}$ By the Rev$^{d}$ John Alcock.

1803.

John the Son of John Downs Yeaman Burid Feby 14$^{th}$ by the Rev$^{d}$ John Alcock.
Ellin the Wife of Henry Ovington Yeaman Burid Feb$^{y}$ 28$^{d}$ by the Rev$^{d}$ John Alcock.
Elliner the Doughter of James Ellis Joyn$^{r}$ Buri$^{d}$ March 16$^{th}$ by the Rev$^{d}$ John Alcock.
Margaret the Doughter of Joseph Lupton Miner Buri$^{d}$ April 11$^{th}$ by Rev$^{d}$ John Alcock.

Mary the Widdow of Henry Ellis Joyner Buri$^{d}$ July 14$^{th}$ by the Rev$^{d}$ John Alcock.

Nancy Middlebrough Opoper Buri$^{d}$ Sept$^{r}$ 9$^{th}$ by the Rev$^{d}$ John Alcock.

Margaret the Widdow of John Whitaker Yeaman Buri$^{d}$

Baptizms 1804. [D fol. 14 v.

Benjamin the Son of James Ellis Joyner Bap$^{d}$ March 30$^{th}$ by R$^{d}$ J. Wilson.

Isable the Doughter of William Wrathall Farmer Bap$^{d}$ April 30$^{th}$ by R$^{d}$ J. Alcock.

Ann the Daughter of William Ibbotson Labou$^{r}$ Bap$^{d}$ May 13$^{th}$ by R$^{d}$ J. A.

Isable the Daughter of William Petty Labour$^{r}$ Bap$^{d}$ May 29$^{th}$ by the R$^{d}$ J. Alcock.

Mary the Daughter of Rich$^{d}$ Stoyls Labour$^{r}$ Bap$^{d}$ July 28$^{th}$ by J. A.

Margaret the Daughter of Step$^{n}$ Wrathall Farmer Bap$^{d}$ Sept$^{r}$ 2$^{nd}$ by R$^{d}$ John Alcock.

Grace the Daughter of Francis Hasleton Farmer Bap$^{d}$ Nov$^{r}$ 4$^{th}$ by the Rev$^{d}$ J. Alcock.

1805.

John the Son of Leonard Sedgswick Farmer Bap$^{d}$ March 23$^{d}$ by the Rev$^{d}$ Bentham.

Elija the Son of Jam$^{s}$ Ellis Joyner Bap$^{d}$ April 7$^{th}$ by the Rev$^{d}$ W$^{m}$ Lister.

Sarah the Daughter of Harman Trueman Innkeeper Borne Sept$^{r}$ 8$^{th}$ Babt$^{d}$ Sept$^{r}$ 15$^{th}$ by the Rev$^{d}$ John Alcock.

James the Son of Henry Whitaker Yeaman Borne Sept$^{r}$ 12$^{th}$ Babt$^{d}$ Sept$^{r}$ 15 by the Rev$^{d}$ W$^{m}$ Lister.

Rich$^{d}$ the Son of Grace Blaco a Basterd Child Born Sept$^{r}$ 28$^{th}$ Bapt$^{d}$ Octob$^{r}$ the 2$^{nd}$ By the Rev$^{d}$ Will$^{m}$ Lister.

Michal the Son of Will$^{m}$ Petty Labour$^{r}$ Born and Bap$^{d}$ Octo$^{r}$ 11$^{th}$ by the R$^{d}$ W$^{m}$ Lister.

George the Son of Stephen Hardaker Farmer Barne Novemb$^{r}$ 21$^{st}$ and Bapti$^{d}$ Novemb$^{r}$ 30$^{th}$ by the R$^{d}$ W$^{m}$ Lister.

1806.

Thomas the Son of John Downs Yeaman Born Janua$^{y}$ 11$^{th}$ Bap$^{d}$ Jan$^{y}$ 27$^{th}$ by Rev$^{d}$ W$^{m}$ Lister.

1805.

Jane the Doughter of John Ellison Farmer Born May 1$^{st}$ Bap$^{d}$ May 5$^{th}$ by R$^{d}$ J. A.

1806.

Sarah Doughter of James Ellis Joyner born April 24$^{th}$ baptized May 20$^{th}$ by the Rev$^{d}$ W$^{m}$ Lister.

Benjamin the Daughter of Francis Hasleton Farmer Born Augu$^{st}$ 24$^{th}$ Bap$^{d}$ Augu 31$^{st}$ b1 R$^{d}$ J. A.

Sarah the Daughter of W$^{m}$ Petty Labou$^{r}$ Born Augu$^{st}$ 29$^{th}$ Bapti$^{d}$ Augu$^{st}$ 31$^{st}$ by R$^{d}$ J. Alcock.

William the Son of W$^{m}$ Ibbotson Labour$^{r}$ Born Decem$^{r}$ 4$^{th}$ Bapti$^{d}$ Dec$^{d}$ 25$^{th}$ by R$^{d}$ J. Alcock.

Mary Ann the Doughter of W$^{m}$ Leytham Labour$^{r}$ born Dec$^{r}$ 28$^{th}$ Baptized Janua$^{y}$ 4$^{th}$ 1807 by the Rev$^{d}$ John Alcock.

1807.

Alice the Daughter of Robert Hallam Farmer March 14th Bapti^d^ April 12th by R^d^ J. Alcock.

Robert the Son of Simon Clark Cordwainer born April 1st baptiz^d^ April 5th by R^d^ J. Wilson.

Mary the Doughter of Harman Trueman Innkeeper born June 25th baptized Sept^r^ 18th by the Rev^d^ John Alcock.

Stephen the Son of James Ellis Joyner Born July 31st Bap^d^ Augu^t^ 9th by R^d^ J. Wilson.

1808.

James the Son of Tho^s^ Ibbotson Labour^r^ born Feb^y^ 4th Bap^d^ Feb^y^ 21st by R^d^ J. Wilson.

Robert the Son Stephen Hardaker Farmer born April 4th bap^d^ Apr^l^ 10th by R^d^ J. Alcock.

Thomas the Son of John Armitstead Inn Keeper born April 17th bap^d^ May 8th by the Rev^d^ John Alcock.

Arebela the Doughter of William Ibbotson Labour^r^ Born June 10th Babtized June 26st by the Rev^d^ John Wilson.

Burials 1803. [D fol. 15 r.

Sarah the Wife of Chris^r^ Atkinson Opo^r^ Buri^d^ Nov^r^ 3^d^ by R^d^ J. Alcock.

1805.

Alice the Wife of Chris^r^ Petty Opo^r^ Buri^d^ Octob^r^ 2nd By Rev^d^ W^m^ Lister.

Michal the Son of Will^m^ Petty Labour^r^ Buri^d^ Octob^r^ 15th by Rev^d^ W^m^ Lister.

Elija the Son of James Ellis Joyner Buri^d^ Decemb^r^ 15th by the Rev^d^ W^m^ Lister.

1806.

Tibby the Daughter of Chris^r^ Atkinson Labou^r^ Buri^d^ Januar^y^ 15th by the Rev^d^ Wm Lister.

Mary the Wife of Rodger Broughton Miner Buri^d^ January 22nd by the Rev^d^ W^m^ Lister.

Mary the Daughter of Christ^r^ Mallinson Labou^r^ Buri^d^ July 27th by the Rev^d^ John Alcock.

Thomas the Son of John Downs yeaman Buri^d^ Sept^r^ 22nd by the Rev^d^ John Alcock.

1807.

Jane the Wife of Will^m^ Leytham Labour^r^ Buri^d^ Jan^y^ 9th by the Rev^d^ John Alcock.

Elizabeth the Doughter of John Downs Farmer Barrows Buri^d^ Feb^y^ 4th by Rev^d^ J. Alcock.

Thomas Tomlinson Opo^r^ Buri^d^ April 9th by the Rev^d^ John Wilson.

Mary Widow of John Holgate Miller Buri^d^ April 18th by the Rev^d^ John Alcock.

James the Son of Henry Whitaker Yeaman Buri^d^ Octo^r^ 15th by the Rev^d^ John Alcock.

Chris^r^ Petty Opo^r^ Buri^d^ Nov^r^ 28th by the Rev^d^ John Alcock.

1808.

Nanny the Widdow of John Needham Miner Buri$^{d}$ July 10$^{th}$ by the Rev$^{d}$ John Alcock.

Mary the Wife of Joseph Tennant Labour$^{r}$ Buri$^{d}$ Sept$^{r}$ 28$^{th}$ by Rev$^{d}$ J. Alcock.

1809.

Margarat Widdow of Henry Constantine Yeaman Buri$^{d}$ Augu$^{t}$ 27$^{th}$ by the Rev$^{d}$ John Alcock.

1810.

Alice the Daugter of Harman Trueman Inn Keeper Burid March 30$^{th}$ by Rev$^{d}$ John Bentham.

Ann the Widdow of Chris$^{r}$ Mallinson Labour$^{r}$ Buri$^{d}$ April 11$^{th}$ by R$^{d}$ John Bentham.

Joseph the Son of Chris$^{r}$ Windle Labour$^{r}$ Buri$^{d}$ Decem$^{r}$ 4$^{th}$ by R$^{d}$ John Bentham.

1811.

Thomasin the Daughter of George Horner Yeaman Buri$^{d}$ Feb$^{y}$ 5$^{th}$ by R$^{d}$ Bland.

Frances the Wife of Richard Holgate Yeaman Buri$^{d}$ March 24$^{th}$ by R$^{d}$ J. Bentham.

Robert the Son of Henry Duckit Labourer Buried June 25$^{th}$ by the Rev$^{nd}$ Steph$^{n}$ Bland.

1812.

Charles Ellis the Son of James Ellis Joiner Buried April 3$^{d}$ by the Rev$^{nd}$ Stephen Bland.

Elizabeth the Daughter of James Ellis Joiner Buried May y$^{e}$ 19$^{th}$ by the Rev$^{d}$ John Bentham.

Ellen the Wife of George Horner Yeaman Buri$^{d}$ Sept$^{r}$ 3$^{d}$ by the Rev$^{d}$ Stephen Bland.

Baptisms 1808. [D fol. 15 v.

Mary Ann the Daughter of Mary Plues a Bastard Child born and Baptized August 7$^{th}$ by the Rev$^{d}$ John Alcock.

Elizabeth the Daughter of Robert Hallam Farmer born Sept$^{r}$ 2$^{nd}$ Baptiz$^{d}$ Sept$^{r}$ 25$^{th}$ by Rev$^{d}$ John Alcock.

Matthew the Son of Francis Hesleton Farmer Born Decem$^{r}$ 30$^{th}$ 1808 Babtized January 13$^{th}$ 1809 by the Rev$^{d}$ John Alcock.

1809.

Thomas the Son of Simon Clark Cordwainer born Feb$^{y}$ 5$^{th}$ baptiz$^{d}$ Feb$^{y}$ 8$^{th}$ by the Rev$^{d}$ John Wilson.

Dorothy the Daugter of Leon$^{d}$ Sidgswick Farmer born Feb$^{y}$ 23$^{d}$ baptiz$^{d}$ Feb$^{y}$ 26$^{st}$ by the Rev$^{d}$ John Alcock.

Alice the Daughter of John Ellison Farmer born March 6$^{st}$ baptiz$^{d}$ March 12$^{th}$ by the Rev$^{d}$ John Alcock.

Henry the Son of John Green Labour$^{r}$ born May 15$^{th}$ baptiz$^{d}$ May 21$^{st}$ by the Rev$^{d}$ John Alcock.

Thomas the Son of Richard Coates Labour$^{r}$ born June 16$^{th}$ baptiz$^{d}$ July 9$^{th}$ by the Rev$^{d}$ John Wilson.

William the Son of W$^{m}$ Petty Labour$^{r}$ born June 19$^{th}$ baptiz$^{d}$ July 2$^{nd}$ by the Rev$^{d}$ John Alcock.

Alice the Daughter of Harman Trueman Inn Keeper born Decem$^{r}$ 9 baptized Dec$^{r}$ 28$^{th}$ by Rev$^{d}$ John Alcock.

1810.

William the Son of Henry Shaw Labour$^{r}$ Baurdley born January 13$^{th}$ Baptized Februa$^{y}$ 4$^{th}$ by the Rev$^{d}$ John Bentham.

Charls the Son of James Ellis Joyner born January 18$^{th}$ Babtized Jan$^{y}$ 28$^{th}$ by the Rev$^{d}$ John Bentham.

Mary the Daughter of Stephen Hardaker Farmer born June 21$^{st}$ baptiz$^{d}$ June 24$^{th}$ by the Rev$^{d}$ John Wilson.

Joseph the Son of Chris$^{r}$ Windle Labour$^{r}$ born Decem$^{r}$ 1$^{st}$ baptiz$^{d}$ Dec$^{r}$ 2$^{nd}$ by the Rev$^{d}$ John Bentham.

1811.

Robert the Son of Francis Hesleton Farmer born Jan$^{y}$ 26$^{th}$ Baptized Feb$^{y}$ 10$^{th}$ by the Rev$^{d}$ John Bentham.

Mary Ann the Daughter of Simon Clark Cordwainer born and baptized Februar$^{y}$ 24$^{th}$ by the Rev$^{d}$ John Bentham.

Robert the Son of William Ibbotson Labour$^{r}$ born March 19$^{th}$ babtized April 7$^{th}$ by the Rev$^{d}$ John Bentham.

Baptisms 1811. [D fol. 16 r.

Westby Newby Shackleton Son of Christopher and Ruth Shackleton born Feb$^{y}$ 4$^{th}$ 1810 baptized about that time, received into the Congregation Sep$^{r}$ 1$^{st}$ 1811 by R. Withnell Rector.

Grace Daughter of Harman and Grace Trueman Innkeeper born July 25$^{th}$ baptized Sep$^{t}$ 2$^{nd}$ 1811 by the Rev$^{d}$ Rich$^{d}$ Withnell Rector of Burnsall.

John the Son of W$^{m}$ and Sarah Petty Labour$^{r}$ born Aug$^{st}$ 29$^{th}$ baptized Sept$^{r}$ 8$^{th}$ 1811 by the Rev$^{nd}$ Stepen Bland.

1812.

John the Son Rich$^{d}$ and Betty Coat Labour$^{r}$ born Feb 10$^{th}$ baptized Feb 23$^{d}$ 1812 by the Rev$^{nd}$ Stephen Bland.

Mary the Daughter of Christopher Windle Labour$^{r}$ born May 23$^{d}$ Baptized June 7$^{th}$ by the Rev$^{d}$ Stephen Bland.

John the Son of John Ellison Farmer born Augu$^{t}$ 6$^{th}$ baptiz$^{d}$ 31$^{st}$ by the Rev$^{d}$ Rich$^{d}$ Withnell Rector.

Richard the Son of Leon$^{d}$ Sidgswick Farmer born Augu$^{t}$ 24$^{th}$ baptiz$^{d}$ 30$^{th}$ by the Rev$^{d}$ Rich$^{d}$ Withnell Rector.

Mary the Daughter of Stephen Smith Collier born Octo$^{r}$ 26$^{th}$ baptiz$^{d}$ Dec$^{r}$ 6$^{th}$ by the Rev$^{d}$ Stephen Bland.

# INDEX OF PLACES.

# INDEX OF NAMES.

www.ingramcontent.com/pod-product-compliance
Lightning Source LLC
Chambersburg PA
CBHW030547270326
41927CB00008B/1548

* 9 7 8 3 3 3 7 4 3 0 3 7 5 *